SAUNA MAGIC

Health ❦ Happiness ❦ Community

Garrett Conover

Sauna Magic
Copyright © 2019 Garrett Conover

ISBN: 978-1-63381-166-9

All rights reserved. No part of this book may be reproduced in any form or by any electronic or mechanical means, including information storage and retrieval systems, without permission in writing from the author, except by a reviewer, who may quote brief passages in review.

Designed and produced by:
Maine Authors Publishing
12 High Street, Thomaston, Maine
www.maineauthorspublishing.com

Printed in the United States of America

For *Sauna Tonttu,*
the spirit that comes to occupy a well-loved, happy sauna

Acknowledgments

Bill Osgood of Vermont initially introduced me to authentic sauna, and undoubtedly reinforced my already developing tendencies with respect for tracking down the origins, history, and stories that cradle any topic. Through Bill, I met his daughter Kati, who happened to share a great many interests in all things northern—natural and cultural history, music, contra dancing, literature, folklore—and who also has a keen interest in sauna. It turned out that Kati was extremely knowledgeable about sauna as practiced in Finland. Not only is she fluent in Finnish, but her PhD is from a Finnish university. After Bill's passing, she returned to the family homestead called Ravencroft, and regularly fires up Hrafn Sauna—*hrafn* being the Icelandic word for "raven." Everything I managed to absorb during my sauna introductory years is due to Bill's early influence, and continues through Kati's knowledge and generosity. Empirically, and as a habitually scholarly person, she provides thorough, detail-rich answers to any questions posed to her, and often additional follow-up. My gratefulness for each of these friendships is boundless. They established a solid foundation that enhances all continuing explorations within the world of sauna.

Wende Nelson and Scott Mills of Ely, Minnesota, are thanked for sending me the first stone for my sauna stove, as well as another from the Agawa pictograph site on the north shore of Lake Superior.

Since I have been working at Sheldon Slate for the past several years I need to thank John Tatko and Jim Wentworth for their tolerance of me dashing off on various research trips related to this project. John deserves additional thanks for unwittingly becoming part of the project twenty-some years earlier when I first built my sauna. I had asked about slate for a spark guard to go in front of the stove, and he immediately became intrigued enough to not only provide the slate and some design suggestions, as well as teach me how to sandblast a design into the center tile, but as a generous friend he never billed me for materials or his efforts.

Those who opened their sauna practice to me and are front and center in the chapters that profile them literally give content, voice, and diversity to this book. Among

1

them are Nils Shenholm, Mary Flemming, Rollin and Andrea Thurlow, Sergei Breus, Bill Morrison, Fred Fauver, and John Pederson. While these people are the primary spokespeople of their chapters, there are many more to thank within their communities who are important to the whole. Everyone mentioned by name in the various chapters falls into this collective, with Glenn Auerbach, Margie Weaver, Max Musicant, Andrea Johnson, Molly Reichert, Sara Hill, Teke O'Reilly, Yukiko Oyama, and Rodney Buhrsmith as stand-out spokespeople and friends. And there are many that appear in the photographs who I may have met only once and whose names I may not have learned. Their willingness to be included has improved everything.

A few of the "sauna regulars" that appear in the imagery are thanked for their willingness to participate in the photography repeatedly over the years. Elisa Schine, Zoey Greenberg, Ann Hurley, Bet Black, Steven Hanton, Merlin and Hannah Knight, Dorcas Sefton, Alexandra Conover Bennett, Kendall Williams, Stephen Carpenter, Allyson Fauver, Pia Capaldi, Elise Becksvoort, Kielyn and David Marrone, and Nikki Wachlarowicz are most heartily thanked for not being shy in this regard. There are also a number of visitors, students, and others who appear via one-time appearances who were enthusiastic participants. Among the regulars, Lucy Atkins is not only thanked by me, but had a most helpful impact on many others. She came up with a single-sentence guideline for how to think about candidly appearing in the images. Her idea: "The easiest way to establish your acceptability guidelines for any image you don't veto is to ask yourself, Would you be comfortable with your parents seeing it, or your colleagues at work, and anyone else you know?"

Lucy's comment addresses directly an aspect that heightens my gratefulness. Because sauna is usually engaged in naturally naked, there are some cultural elements that everyone appearing in the text and imagery has transcended. All accept that some people find sauna culture strange, and that some may be offended or uncomfortable, or will view natural bodies voyeuristically. To a person, everyone involved in this book has acknowledged this negative potential with grace and with confidence that it is a very small subset with minimal impact relative to the vast majority who regard sauna with reverence and assume the sanctity of sauna is never compromised. My hope is that our faith in this will be rewarded with acceptance and ultimately not be regarded as a big deal. All of us involved trust that the open, honest, egalitarian nature of sauna will make any initial surprise fade into such a realm of normalcy as to be unremarkable. Should such a thing occur in a reader by the end of the book, it will mirror the process of becoming a comfortably unfettered sauna reveler in person.

Luminaries in the world of sauna who were inspired enough to provide cover endorsements include Carita

Harju, Glenn Auerbach, John Pederson, and Mikkel Aaland. Mikkel was not only generous with his enthusiasm, but was kind enough to suggest some editorial tightening that make the very first paragraphs more inclusive and nuanced to "get this stuff right."

Jane Karker and her team at Maine Authors Publishing is thanked for their professionalism on all fronts. Editor Jane Eklund, designer Michelle Hodgdon, as well as Jenn Dean and Dan Karker were instrumental in guiding every aspect of this book into being.

When Alix Hopkins appeared, this project was well underway, and as our orbits began to overlap and merge, she embraced sauna life in one exuberant swoop. As a writer and photographer herself, her "fresh eyes," support, and guidance have been extraordinarily beneficial. In addition to her editorial observations and ideas, she appears in a number of images and contributed others as photographer.

Infinite thanks to all, Garrett

CHAPTER 1

A Most Wondrous Tradition

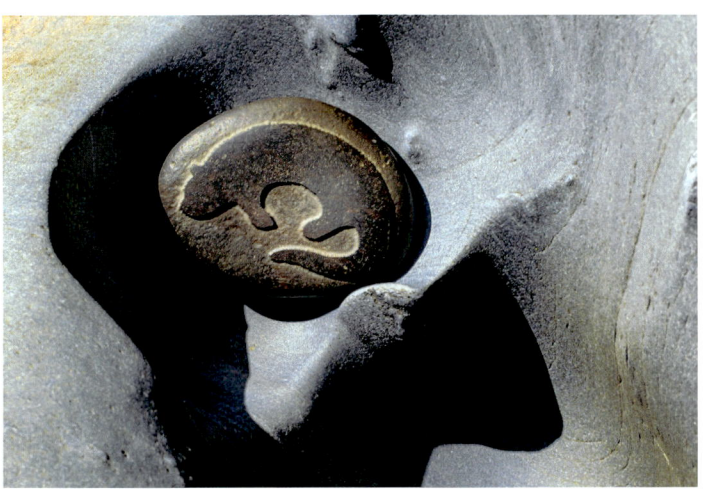

Before falling under the spell of the Finnish style of sweat bath, the sauna, I became inspired by the sweat bath of the Native Americans often referred to as the sweat lodge. This was strictly influence from description and taking part in the sweat lodges of friends who had likewise been influenced. Intuitively, since my experimentation lacked any invitation, my approach was one of care and respect, as most references acknowledged ceremonial and sacred aspects. Indeed the very nature of preparing the lodge, the fire, and rocks, and finally the experience of the sweat, all foster such feelings and appreciation for a far bigger picture. And it is a good place to start. It seems that most cultures all over the world had some form of sweat bathing, and from such origins all the variations and refinements for ritualized bathing share common ground. Sweat lodges are still a thriving part of many traditions, and the various names of more permanent sweat bathing structures roll off the tongue reflecting many languages. In Finnish it is *sauna*, in Russian *banya*, Lithuanian *pirtis*, Swedish and Norwegian refer to *bastu* or *badstue*. In the Middle East there is the *hammam*, in Mexico the *temescal*, and Japan the *mushi-buro*. While architecture and ritual varies, all have much in common regarding ceremonial sense, the physiology of extreme relaxation, purification, and resulting sense of serene well-being.

There was a period where the sweat lodge factored perfectly into my world. My partner at the time, Alexandra, and I were canoe and snowshoe guides leading wilderness trips in Maine, Quebec, and Labrador. When we were just starting out we were caretakers for an absentee owner of a log cabin nestled in a mature spruce woods. There was a surplus of dead and blown-down wood for bonfires for the heating of rocks, and it was easy to make a lodge frame and cover it with canvas tarps. During that time we would fire up any Saturday afternoon we were home, and whichever of the "Saturday sweaters" was available would come over with contributions to a potluck supper. Anywhere from two to ten of us would take a sweat and time it so we'd

Transferring rocks heated to glowing translucent orange from fire to sweat lodge on the shore of Winokapau Lake, Labrador. (Photo by Alexandra Conover Bennett)

finish up, get dressed, and start supper just as the weekly *Prairie Home Companion* broadcast would commence on Public Radio.

It was heavenly. In the soft glow of candles and a couple of Aladdin kerosene lamps, with the radio powered by a car battery and the woodstove crackling in the background, we would settle in with our food in a relaxed and euphoric state while the show's music and stories and skits would transport us all over a marvelous world.

While the caretaker situation lasted only a few years, the canoe trips kept the potential for taking a sweat now and then an ever-present possibility. Sooner or later there would be a wind-bound day on some big lake or a voluntary layover day in a particularly nice spot. Sweat lodge ingredients are everywhere in North Woods canoe country, and on any canoe trip there are always a number of tarps and tent flies that can be pressed into service to cover a lodge.

It was a very small step from the joys of sweat lodges to the equally full magic of Finnish sauna by the time fates, friends, and good luck conspired with invitations and introductions.

While many countries embrace sauna in one form or another, Finland has set the standards against which all other sauna cultures are measured. Finland and sauna are essentially synonymous. Some of us may have become aware of Nokia cell phones when that technology burst upon the scene, been exposed to Sami culture through *National Geographic*, and perhaps are aware of some magnificent accordion music, but these icons of Finland are completely overshadowed by sauna. For the more than 5.8 million people in Finland, the presence of 3 million saunas highlights just how important sauna truly is. There are more saunas than cars. No other place seems to have such a rich folklore surrounding a theme or devoted so much scientific thought and study to a topic or lavished so much love and refinement on something that is paradoxically a common, unremarkable part of any day and also symbolic of life itself. There

Supremely experienced wilderness paddler and winter traveler Wendy enjoys a sweat while windbound on the Atikonak watershed in Labrador.

is a saying that pretty much covers everything physical, mental, and spiritual: "If whatever ails you cannot be cured by sauna, then there is no hope."

Because of its importance and the reverence surrounding it, any effort to pronounce sauna correctly will be appreciated and rewarded. If you simply read the word and apply English phonetics you will inevitably say "sawna." This is not proper. The *a* and *u* need to get their share of the word with a combined hint of each vowel in evidence. If you say "sow-na," you will be quite close, especially if you stretch the first syllable out a bit while pronouncing the a and u much as they sound in the word *sauerkraut*. *Sauna* is literally the only Finnish word to be incorporated into English unaltered, and as such deserves the respect afforded by proper pronunciation.

Sauna is beautiful because it is spare and elemental. Wood, stone, fire, and water are given uninterrupted voice. Ritual follows naturally and spontaneously. Care is required in the building of the structure, as well as the preparations for each use once built. Time is required to accomplish everything properly, and this is important. This is time aside, slow time, full time, and it is rich. No matter how physically demanding, at what pace or level of stress your other activities may have been beforehand, you are now preparing to enter a realm of deep relaxation and bliss.

If the sauna is wood-fired, there is wood to carry, split, and make ready. There may be buckets to fill and water to haul. Tiny as the room may be, it will take an hour or more to "season" or "cure." This is not simply a room holding hot air. The structure itself must be heated; it must be re-radiating a profound, fundamental, encompassing deep heat. Once this state is achieved throughout the walls, floor, ceiling, and benches, the stones cradled by the stove will be fantastically alive with an indescribable intensity of pure hot radiance.

When the thermometer registers 180 to 200 degrees F, many people consider it time to enter. Traditionally,

Fetching spring water for drinking, and river water for a cooling scrub and rinse.

The anticipation and approach to a ready sauna is as important as all other elements of preparation and enjoying. Each step becomes a thoughtful, ceremonial part of the whole. An esthetic setting, mostly natural materials, and bare feet on the trail all build resonance.

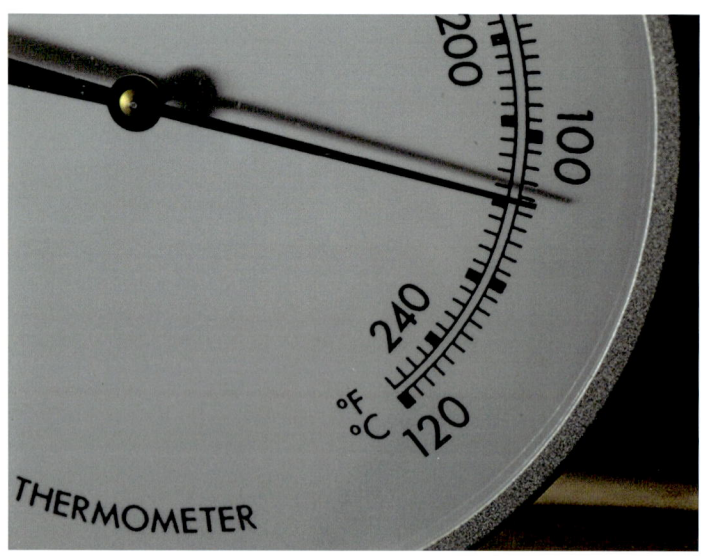

A sauna thermometer mounted at bench height indicates readiness and preferred heat levels.

True stream crackles forth invisibly from properly hot stones, releasing negative ions. Too much visible vapor indicates rocks that are not hot enough for optimum rewards.

sauna is experienced naked, and this indeed is best. You will sit quietly for a while and let your body respond. Extreme heat is different than whatever level of heat and humidity might make us uncomfortable and irritable in our ambient environments. There is something magical and rewarding about the intense heat of sauna. Breathing slows; your skin expands and opens and begins to flow. There is a great purging of mind and body, and a deepening sense of relaxation. After ten or fifteen minutes, someone may sprinkle a dipper of water over the stones.

If the stones are properly hot—and they are if you entered when the room was over 180 degrees—there will be no visible vapor produced when they are sprinkled. True steam will crackle forth and release negative ions. This is the magical part of sauna, and much of the essence arises from this process. *Löyly* is the Finnish word for this, and it is as difficult to translate as it is for English speakers to pronounce. The term encompasses everything to do with the intense radiating heat from the rocks, the transformation of water to invisibility, and the total infusion of spiritual essences and symbols as the bathers are enveloped by a physical and mystical process. English is not a language that favors conjuring complex knowledge or description when a world-view is equal parts spiritual, scientific, and mythical. It reflects a preference for separation rather than confluence. Fortunately, in the quiet suspended time of sauna, even those who prefer a compartmentalized mind usually respond to the empirical marvels of *löyly* with willing abandon.

Should English speakers wish to attempt saying *löyly* despite the difficulties, you can achieve an approximation. While one source suggests that saying "loo loo" is close enough, it isn't. The *ö* part might best be attempted as a slurring of *e* and *u* into a single but ever-so-slightly stretched vowel that blends both, as if you were enunciating the first two letters of *Europe*, or the middle letters of the name *Fleur*. Next, you need a hint of a syllable that isn't really there, but sounds like a short *i*. Follow this with "loo" for the final *ly*. Phonetically, it might appear like this: leu-i loo. Only if you successfully stretch the first syllable, nearly swallow the second out of existence but leave a hint, and then say *loo* as you would, will a Finnish speaker have any idea what you are trying to say. The word is a perfect mirror of the ethereal difficulties associated with it. For English speakers, it can't quite be said, can't quite be translated, and defines something that can't quite be comprehended. It's like dancing with an enchanting ghost.

The negative ions enhance the heightened euphoria that seems to embrace each reveler, and the steam will condense on everyone, making the skin feel hotter and adding moisture to the process of sweating. Even with the sprinkling of water the overall humidity will stay relatively low, and this no doubt explains why such intense heat remains inexplicably comfortable and rewarding. The frequency with which the stones are sprinkled is a matter of individual taste, and there will be some variation here. Experience will teach what individual preferences are.

After a while, a threshold of heat tolerance will be reached and you will need to go out and cool. There may be buckets of water outside to pour over heads and backs, a lake or stream to cool in, or, in the case of some indoor saunas, a handy shower to cool under. Even in summer, simply cooling in the air will work, although radical cooling via water over the head is preferable and may be necessary. In winter, air cooling is plenty fine and fast. If it is much below zero F, the tips of your hair may freeze before your skin registers anything but the heat it is radiating. You need to discern a chill before reentering the sauna for additional sessions. For the ultimate contrast a roll in powder snow or a quick dip through a hole cut in lake ice are worth experiencing for the unlikely humor, extreme curiosity, or just to have done it, but neither is necessary for adequate cooling, nor is either, for many, a routine part of sauna.

While many people simply bask quietly during each heating session and rinse during the cooling sessions between, others enjoy a good scrub during the first cooling session with a bath brush or loofa sponge to fully exfoliate, clean deeply, and then follow with a thorough rinse. Having your own dedicated bucket facilitates this, but if there is a basin of cooling water shared by everyone, make sure you apply water and rinse any brushes or sponges with a dipper, away from and not in the communal water.

Birch vihta for improving circulation by whisking yourself or your companions and introducing a lovely scent to the hot room and your skin.

Once rinsed, your skin will flow even more freely, and your tolerance will rise for longer heating sessions. If there are bundles of leafy birch twigs (*vihta* or *vasta* in Finnish, depending on the region) present you can gently whisk yourself to improve circulation and stimulate the skin. In winter you might try bringing a snowball back in with you. A snowball gently traced over your skin is particularly wonderful as the heat of the next session engulfs you. Collarbones, shoulders, thighs, sternum, eyelids, and cheekbones seem exceptionally delighted by the snowball treatment. As spring arrives and repeated thaw and freeze cycles create granular "corn" snow, another glorious snow feature emerges. Scrubbing with a handful of corn snow combines cooling with a comfortable yet abrasive exfoliating scrub that is self-lubricating,

Pre-soaking a vihta in the river to rehydrate for use, a process which can also be done in a basin of warm water if the vihta has been dried for use in winter.

contours perfectly, provides a simultaneous rinse, and vanishes when done. Usually any given sauna will involve a number of heating and cooling sessions and you will feel "done" after an hour and a half or so. Or, as one friend who enjoys exaggeration says, "You're cooked perfectly as soon as you can tie an overhand knot in your femur."

After a final cooling it is time to gently return to ambient conditions. Perhaps a cup of tea, snack, or even a meal is enjoyed. A short sauna session may invigorate you for whatever is next if it is taken early in the day, while afternoon or evening sauna is usually planned and reserved as a full luxurious affair. If timed so you are simply going to bed afterwards, you will slide into a profound and wondrous slumber of unusual quality.

Joints and muscle aches will have vanished even as the sauna sessions progressed. And your skin will feel magic and without specific dimension well into the next day. If you have used birch *vihtas* you may catch an occasional whiff of birch oil still on your skin ten or twenty hours later. After your first introduction you will know if you are giddy and infatuated with sauna, or if you are among those who simply do not care for it. There does not seem to be a middle ground. Most of us not raised within the tradition seem to enter a state of wonder that leaves us reeling and amazed that we didn't know about sauna sooner. There is simply nothing else that offers so many superlative positives and not a single negative. The

During winter sauna, a snowball traced upon the skin makes a lively contrast to the intense heat.

physical and health benefits are legion, as are the psychological, familial, social, and community building aspects, not to mention the abundance of simple, pure

Awakening to a soft summer dawn from the profoundly deep slumber following a sauna the evening before.

Guest room, cooling room, and sauna in the basement of a home in Ely, Minnesota.

Combined guest cabin and sauna on Lake Vermilion, Minnesota.

pleasure that is delivered. Any single point is worthy of unabashed obsession, and the full aggregate is nothing short of miraculous. We might find ourselves driving acquaintances nutty with a gushy enthusiasm for our "discovery." What a gift! What an amazing thing! Why doesn't everyone know about this? Why don't the Finns tell *everybody*? We learn soon enough to calm down, enjoy the secret, and let it be. You either get it or you don't; the experience can't be adequately told.

In North America it was easy to trace the different waves of Finnish immigration across the landscape by the presence of saunas. Before the advent of electrically heated units that are now usually inside the main house, the family sauna was a small, tight outbuilding. To the wonder of non-comprehending neighbors, the sauna was often the first structure put up on a homestead, or a small cabin did double duty as a home and sauna while barns and other structures were built, and eventually a house could be built and occupied.

With a few exceptions, immigration from Finland came relatively late in the European peopling of North America. Unlike the founding groups that suffered from a feverish zeal to recreate pastoral Europe from the dense forests of the northeastern wilderness, the Finns were not terrified of the wilds or the habitat, and unlike the New England Puritans, they were mercifully free of a theology that equated naturalness and wildness with godlessness. In fact, the landscapes the Finns gravitated to had all the comforts of home, especially the familiar boreal forests. The Finnish people were used to hard work in marginal landscapes, and quite at home making do with what was available. Where earlier occupiers had cleared the readily farmable land, the Finns could see potential in overlooked places. Many had a well-developed stubborn independence that could make such places yield what was required. This habitual grit and tenacity of purpose is called *sisu*, and is a point of pride. If people had enough *sisu* to look on these leftover lands favorably and as desirable, they might also have a differing set of priorities regarding the order and importance of which buildings went up first. If the comforts of sauna were attended to, the rest would follow in due course.

Johnnie Aho sauna returning to the soil from which it was hewn, the last building left on the Aho homestead site in Monson, Maine.

In addition to homesteading potential, certain cash economies were attractive to those from Finland. There was always work to be had quarrying granite on the coasts, slate in inland Maine, and marble, slate, and granite in Vermont and New York. Nickel, copper, and iron mining replaced quarrying across Ontario and the northern Midwest. Logging work was available in the north woods and all the way westward. More often than not, clusters of Finnish communities in northern regions are in the vicinity of these types of opportunity, although a sprinkling of millwork in Massachusetts and southern New Hampshire seems to have been an equally powerful magnet. In many regions the autonomous small farmsteads proved more stable in the long run, while factories and labor-driven resource extraction industries reflected the boom-and-bust cycles that punctuate much of history.

In the tiny central Maine town of Monson there is yet a high percentage of Finns. Nearly a hundred years have passed since the beginnings of the slate quarrying that brought them here, but farming and forestry continue to provide opportunities. There are a number of active saunas in town, and an equal number returning to the soil in long-abandoned fields now being reclaimed by woods. Far more visible to the outsider's eye than the discreet presence of saunas is what is locally known as the "Finn Hall." Just south of town on the main road is a small, tidy dance hall where on many a Saturday night in summer the sound of fiddles and accordions ring out, playing the schottisches, waltzes, and polkas popular in Finland at the time the most recent wave of immigrants started arriving in the 1930s. The oldest dancers can still be heard "talking Finn" among themselves, and the revival of pride and interest in cultural heritage has given a bit of new life to the dance hall beyond the Finnish community. Where a newcomer might expect the name of such a place to reflect the local quarrying history, the sign above the door simply says "Finnish Farmers Club." Among the true Finns on the dance floor, the music, *sisu*, and sauna are undiminished, while in the surrounding hills the number of slate quarries has dwindled from dozens in the region to only one active enterprise.

Legend has it that the house accordionist, Jorma Ranta (you must roll the *r*'s lustily), played for forty-five years without missing a single dance following the founding of the Finn Hall in 1935. And the legend is not too far from the truth, not only because Jorma was a tireless musician who knew the Finnish dance tunes, but because he was among those who brought the Finn Hall back to life after many years of dormancy. What the legend leaves out to enhance the storytellers' impact is that there was an extended period when the hall was essentially abandoned and there were no dances for the accordionist to miss. But Jorma remembered the importance of the dance, and in his final years helped revive it as a community event.

Metsalaulu, or Woodsong, keeps the Monson Finn Hall dances lively.

17

Bill Osgood, the former librarian for the Center for Northern Studies, named his sauna in Vermont at Ravencroft with the Icelandic word for Raven.

At the Northern Comfort Lodge in Embarrass, Minnesota, the sauna log reflects the original farm family's Finnish roots.

When Bill's daughter, Kati Osgood, inherited the farmstead, she put her experience living in Finland, and fluency in the language, into a direct reflection of influences.

Fortunately, before passing on, he influenced a few local musicians who have carried the sound forward as a band named Metsalaulu (Woodsong), and they in turn are encouraging other musicians to learn the particulars of the Finnish lilt and tempos. Every so often there is a special treat when accordionist Veikko Honkela drives five hours north from Ashburnham, Massachusetts, to play the Finn Hall with the same authority and authenticity as Jorma.

Jorma's home, just over the crest of Tenney Hill from the Finn Hall, is now occupied by his grandson, Billy. Every so often I see smoke coming from the sauna stovepipe, and I like to imagine it contains a hint of Jorma, a gesture in the sky to freshen memory.

Travel westward from New England, following the transition lands between farming to the south and forest to the north, and you will find plenty of Finns. When you reach the northern Midwest and the Great Lakes basin, you might think you've been mysteriously transported to Finland itself. Saunas, the "sign of the Finn," are everywhere. You might even find yourself in Finland, Minnesota, just west and north of the far shore of Lake Superior. While "Little Finlands" can be found in many places, Ontario, Michigan, Wisconsin, and Minnesota form the cradle of Finnish culture in North America. Not surprisingly, here where the density and numbers are highest, sauna culture is much less mysterious and not so likely to be regarded as strange. Several of the sauna stove manufacturers are in this region, and in places like Duluth and Ely, Minnesota, and Thunder Bay and Sudbury, Ontario, you can find whole shops devoted to sauna equipment and accessories, as well as some renowned public saunas. As with many things, familiarity is a great ambassador, and this wondrous gift from the Finns is now embraced widely by extremely grateful people from all sorts of places and walks of life.

While many are introduced to sauna at a public sauna or a sauna in a motel or sports complex, it is likely that such an experience will be incomplete, leaving you with unanswered questions—and may, in fact, be lacking impact and resonance. To fully experience sauna, express your interest to someone who has one or who can be your guide to a quality public sauna that measures up to Finnish ideals. Most owners are enthusiastic and are likely to reward genuine interest with an invitation. For many, not offering sauna to guests would be considered rather unaccommodating and even impolite.

Once invited, inquire what the host family or organization's protocols are. This will relieve any uncertainties you may have and put your hosts at ease by allowing them direct opportunity to communicate and instruct. While natural nakedness is best, it can be quite a hurdle for some North Americans to leap in a single bound. Fear not. There are various solutions. Some hosts will

A kerosene lantern hanging outside illuminates both the cooling deck and interior.

offer to wrap themselves in a towel or wear a swimsuit if that would add to your comfort. Others may invite you to cover as much as you wish, even though they may be naked. You may be offered a same-gender experience or even invited to take your introductory sauna by yourself after being given instructions. Those not raised within the tradition have no empirical knowledge or experiential assumptions regarding the safety and sanctity of sauna, so that must be seamlessly and sensitively part of the introduction to newcomers.

The sauna room will typically be small for ease of heating, and may have a changing room or a deck for entry. There will be a stove or heater inside and a series of benches, usually at two or more levels—the upper being hotter and the lowest cooler. The spare, clean lines are very soothing. A few buckets, ladles, and perhaps some leafy birch twig *vihtas* may be present. A thermometer is likely to be mounted at bench height to reference readiness at a preferred heat level.

Lighting is usually subtle, and just enough for safety around the stove. Many log or frame saunas will have only one small window to admit light during the day and a place for a kerosene lantern to be hung outside after dark so that the light will pass through the window and illuminate the interior while any fumes disperse safely. If electricity is available, lighting is a simple matter, and with all sorts of solar and battery powered LED lights now available, safety and esthetics are easily achieved.

Most lighting suppliers have a variety of mood lighting options in all colors, as well as lights that realistically mimic the subtle flickering and softness of candles or a kerosene lamp, but without fumes, melting wax, or danger from an open flame. Ambience and safety are the concerns. Fostering this sense of calm is as important as every other aspect of sauna, and is very similar to how a campfire might enhance the feelings of tribal or familial communion among those gathered around.

Candles in the changing room flicker through a stained-glass window at the Bob Henderson sauna on Smoke Lake in Ontario.

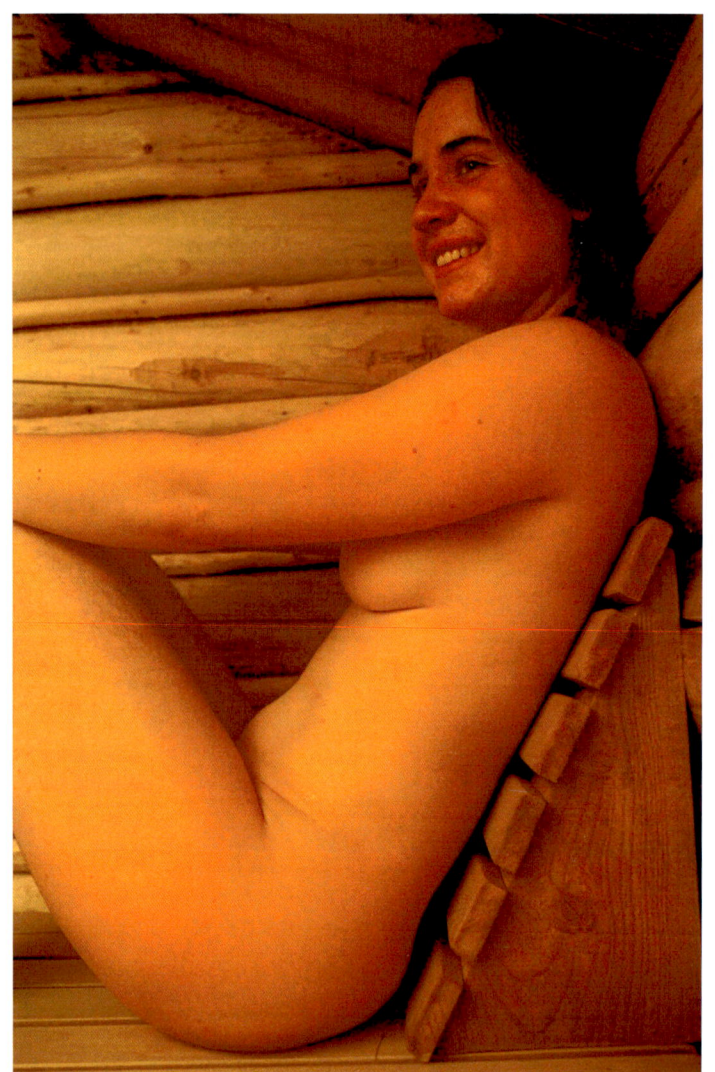 

A bench rest oriented vertically supports the back; horizontally, it becomes a rest for head and shoulders.

You might bring a towel to sit on and perhaps your own small basin and scrub brush. Drinking water should be available in the cooling area, and many bring water into the sauna itself.

For your first experience, you may want to enter when the thermometer registers 175 or 180 degrees F. Over time you will likely discover that your personal preference falls somewhere within the 180-to-220 degree range, with higher temperatures best reserved for the blasting of cold or flu symptoms but not prolonged basking. Upon opening the door to enter, any clean sauna will greet you with an incredibly rich fragrance that combines the infused essence of hot, unfinished, aromatic wood of the benches and room sheathing, the dry heat of the stones, and perhaps the spicy freshness of essential oil droplets that may have been added to the water to be sprinkled on the rocks. Although you probably wouldn't anticipate this sensual welcome being of major importance on your introductory sauna, you will come to anticipate it keenly. Indeed, it becomes an important aspect of each experience that never diminishes in impact.

Take a low bench at first until you gain familiarity with the heat and the feel, and become comfortable. You will know how long to bask, when to go out to cool off, and when to try a higher bench. Your body will tell you, and initially this will be influenced by your state of mind. Once any uncertainties fade and you can surrender fully to the event, you will discover that a profound and satisfying level of bliss is a usual and achievable state.

Wood-heated saunas are by far a superior experience. Both the higher temperature potential and quality of the heat are markedly different. But don't be discouraged if an electric or propane-fired sauna is what is available. It may still be magical. Most are slightly cooler, and may not get the rocks hot enough for negative ion release, but you will still get hot and sweat profusely and well enough to achieve the euphoric feelings of deep cleanliness and relaxation, along with the sense of being purged. Some public saunas are kept even cooler to accommodate a wide range of people with unknown preferences. The trick in places where you can't personally control the heat is to manage your expectations. A sub-optimum experience (unless the temperature drops below 160 degrees F) is still better than no sauna at all.

The frequency with which water is ladled on the stones is very much a personal preference. Over time you will settle on what is best for you. Some are content with a single sprinkle per heating session, while others might like two or three. Whether you like a few spare sprinklings over an hour or more, or six or ten, it is best to tip the dipper slowly and evenly in a pattern that moves water to fresh hot stones for maximum effect. While it can't be done too little, it can be overdone, so experiment cautiously. A long-handled dipper will keep the sprinkler's hand safely away from the sudden jolt of rising steam.

Essential oils for mixing into sprinkling water. (Photo by Alexandra Conover Bennett)

If the sprinkling water is heated in advance it won't cool the rocks as much, and they will return to the full blast of radiance that much quicker. In addition, you can prepare the water with a few drops of fragrant oil for releasing a pleasing scent when it crackles on the stones. Mint, eucalyptus, wintergreen, various evergreen tree scents, birch, and citrus are popular and available at sauna supply shops and in the essential oil racks of health food stores.

Sauna is a place for stories, and perhaps some songs, conversation, or just quiet meditative basking. This happens naturally and spontaneously, but occasionally there might be a need to deliberately disengage from a topic should it evolve toward emotional heat or

argumentativeness. Sauna is not the place for that, for any form of complaining, profanity, or even loud voices.

Being naked enhances all the effects of sauna. Not only does your skin respond evenly and directly to the heat, your circulation and capillary functions perform at optimum levels. Swimsuits are comparatively uncomfortable and restrictive; wrapped towels are better, but still block the process. If necessary, treat these as transitional items that free your mind of inhibitions during your introduction, or reserve them for those public saunas that may have published rules regarding coverage. Most people seem to arrive at the natural best state unconsciously and appreciate it as not just a bit better

The first session in the heat is usually quiet, meditative, and focused inward. It is during the next alternations of heating and cooling sessions that topics and stories emerge. Sauna folk seem naturally inclined to be philosophers or poets and eager to converse and laugh.

While it is proper to be naked in sauna, not everyone is immediately comfortable with that. It is easy enough for everyone to be towel wrapped or in a swimsuit in public saunas with rules for coverage, or in deference to a shy participant

An intermediate option is for individuals to choose some coverage or not, as personal comfort dictates.

If one becomes a sauna regular it usually does not take long to become at ease with and prefer the natural and best experience.

than being covered, but a quantum leap into an entirely different realm of experience. People who may have started out tightly clutching their towel and feeling self-conscious can't even remember when they just let it slip away as too much interference and bother. Shy people have come back from a cooling session having shed a swimsuit and reenter with such grace that few even notice the change, marking arrival at a new level of ease.

Finally, a few notes on being careful. Remember to be cautious around the stove. In the confines of such a small room, it is always close by. Some people install wooden rails around the stove to prevent accidental contact, and in some areas zoning may require such safeguards, especially in public saunas. Remember that anything metal, even jewelry, might get hot enough to burn. While thin earring wires may not absorb enough heat to be noticeable, larger pieces, such as bracelets or necklace components, can become blister-raising hot. Favor wooden or plastic buckets over metal for the same burn avoidance reasons. Leave cups and drinking water containers at the lowest bench or floor level to avoid allowing them to get too hot.

Occasionally you can be surprised by a blast of *löyly* that you didn't anticipate, or perhaps an enthusiastic sprinkler overdoes it. Should a burst be too hot to breathe comfortably, simply cup your hands over your mouth and nose as a breathing shield for the few seconds it takes for the blast to dissipate. This isn't as bad as it may sound, and

Wooden buckets and ladles are not only iconic but are cooler to the touch and won't burn anyone during use.

passes quickly. Move carefully when it is dark or crowded to avoid bumping anyone hard enough to disrupt their balance or nudge them too close to the stove. A sense of polite caution goes a long way in maintaining harmony.

If in your introductory sampling of sauna you should discover that you simply do not respond positively to the experience, it is a simple matter to excuse yourself and retreat to a cooler area. This is nothing to be ashamed of, and it's not worth pushing yourself beyond your comfort level just because your companions think everything is so marvelous. All of us understand that there are those for whom the heat is unpleasant, the small dim confines and unfamiliar extremes may induce a feeling of claustrophobia, or for any number of reasons may be begging for an immediate exit. Should any of that occur, a speedy exit is exactly the proper response.

It is best to eat a full meal after sauna rather than before. Wait at least an hour after a meal before engaging with the heat. If for social ordering of the event it is smoother to share a meal beforehand, simply plan an hour or more of visiting and conversation time following the meal before entering. However, if you can plan for the meal to follow the final cooling period after sauna, you are in for a real treat. Your ability to discern flavors is so improved by sauna as to make the blandest fare sparkle with exotic brightness.

You will need to re-hydrate with plenty of water. You must replace what transpires away, and it is not

Flavor perception is vastly enhanced for a meal that follows sauna, and you will still feel ethereal and without dimension for quite a while.

Drink plenty of water before, during, and following sauna.

Eight-month-old Merlin enjoying his first sauna. Warm water in a basin on the floor is much cooler than the temperature in the room at bench height, allowing parents to enjoy the full heat of the firing.

overdoing things to have ready access to drinking water during sauna. You definitely want to drink a lot afterwards. To not attend to this may invite a dehydration headache soon afterward, or certainly by the following morning. Many have reported that such headaches are akin to a hangover. Far better to be preventative and sip water frequently throughout sauna and afterwards.

Remember that children and young teens have high surface-to-mass ratios. They will need to cool off more frequently than adults, and usually self-select the lower bench levels or even the floor. Infants are best introduced within a large basin at floor level. A basin with warm water is considerably cooler than the temperature of the sauna, so infants can be present without compromising the temperatures favored by adults. Or you can simply include them in the bath before full temperatures are reached.

Welcome to the world of traditional sauna. In the following chapters you will meet various saunas and their people. A range of styles and stories will emerge. For the already experienced sauna reveler, there will be an enthused embrace as each chapter shares its vision. For the newcomer, there will be a wealth of ideas for dreaming your own ceremonial senses into being.

In sauna we are beautifully honest, equal, and at peace. Diverse as we may be, in sauna we celebrate the tribe.

CHAPTER 2

Afterglow at Solhem Sauna

Nils Shenholm keeps a house, shop, and sauna at the crest of a hill on a dirt road in Duxbury, Vermont. Spectacularly crafted sauna building is his trade. He does not like to disappoint, knows the reasons he chooses not to, and has evolving opinions he's happy to back up with careful thoughtfulness. Given a choice, he favors traditional sauna over the interior designs that have become prevalent in the U.S. His work is steeped in radiant wood, subtle lighting, craftsmanship, and the engagement of the senses.

Duxbury is one of those communities tucked into the hill country that defines so much of Vermont, the sort of place that fulfills the calendar and *Yankee* magazine images of quintessential New England. The bigger rivers swing between broad alluvial meadows of rich soil, while their tributaries tumble from steep wooded and boulder-dotted valleys. Above all, the namesake Green Mountains (*Vert Mont*) keep the skylines interesting. The net effect is a tame and occupied landscape with just enough wildness around the edges and at elevation to appeal without being intimidating.

The surrounding area is Cabot Cheese and Ben and Jerry's Ice Cream country, so local dairy farming enjoys more stability than the generally beleaguered industry does outside the region. Cows are everywhere. River bottom farms grow the silage to keep the dairy herds strong, and a number of ski areas, resorts, nonprofits, entrepreneurs, and Jack and Jill's of all trades keep everything else going. It is a vibrant place to be.

When I met Nils in person, we paused in the middle of the road that passes between his home and shop. "Well, this is it" he said, "the World Headquarters of Solhem Sauna." It was crisp and cool after a siege of rain with the colors of fall in the hardwoods as good as they get. Geese were passing musically overhead, and a small brook chuckled and tumbled along the edge of the cleared portions of the property. My impression was that it was an incredibly nice world occupied by someone happy to be charming with a bit of humor.

Earlier in his career, Nils was a restoration carpenter of historic buildings, keeping them period-specific and

33

Nils Shenholm, the Vermont sauna builder.

true to origins and traditions. With the coming of the interstate highway and, a generation later, the internet, the potential to work from home at a pleasing remove from urban business centers, and even the larger Vermont towns of Montpelier and Burlington, appealed to a wave of newcomers seeking the best of rural values and peace and quiet in proximity to recreational opportunities in semi-wild country. Without the periodic influx of people buying hill farms and breathing life into such properties, thousands upon thousands of hewn homesteads and grand barns would have sagged back into the soil from neglect. By the happenstance of timing and skill, Nils was among those in ready demand by new arrivals, many of whom had an interest in preserving the historic homes and outbuildings of their adopted landscape.

At some point Nils built himself a sauna, and this prompted requests from others who also wanted one built. Soon enough he had to make a decision about what his primary "job" was. He became a sauna builder. That was more than twenty-five years ago. Maybe he didn't set out to create a bit of a niche, but one evolved around him nonetheless. He already had a client base familiar with his work, so he made the leap from one keen woodworking interest to an even more passionate one—Finnish sauna. Given the presence of alpine ski areas and a growing number of Nordic skiing facilities, there were plenty of ties to northern European traditions in the area already. Sauna was not an unfamiliar tradition, and demand materialized for Nils and his enterprise.

Solhem Sauna requires a few things for success. There needs to be a base of source materials for the building process. In addition to the usual large-scale building supply outlets, a number of local sawmills can provide specialty woods cut from local woodlots. Nils takes extra pleasure whenever he knows the wood products are harvested sustainably from well-managed woodlots, especially when he knows the foresters, loggers, and sawyers personally. Delivery and shipping costs of raw materials are reduced, local micro-economies are sustained, and quality of the highest sort is kept in sight and achieved. Good practical stuff from the ground close to home.

The name Shenholm lacks the run-on syllables and paired consonants that are often the hallmark of Finnish surnames. This is because it is Swedish. Honoring those roots, the first name in the company moniker is Swedish. *Solhem* means sun home. There are a couple of reasons the second word in the name, *Sauna*, is Finnish. It is more familiar to English speakers and is in fact the most widely recognized Finnish word in English. It is not only descriptively more familiar than the Swedish equivalent, *bastu*, but reflective of Nils's belief regarding the Finnish sauna as the icon and apex of all things related to such traditions.

While many of us might not discern differences between Swedish *bastu*, Russian *banya*, and Finnish sauna, when Nils follows his research interests to the old country it is to visit the museums devoted to Finnish sauna that are on Finnish soil and the builders, foresters, craftsmen, and bathers who are in Finland. He occupies a seat on the board of directors of the North American Sauna Society, and when he orders the stoves for his saunas it is from the Helo Group LTD of Finland, which has a U.S. plant in Minnesota.

Standard Solhem Sauna standalone, fully ready to fire and deliverable on a tilt-bed truck.

To say that Nils is a meticulous craftsman is a bit of an understatement. He is an exacting artist. His work is infused with a vast understanding of context, history, technique, properties of wood, all the senses, and what simply works best and is often unique to sauna. He understands every aspect and detail that leads toward maximizing the gifts of what the sauna as a building is, and what sauna as a process can offer. He has indeed earned the statement that appears below the company name. It states factually and simply: "The Vermont Sauna Builder Since 1990."

There are some signature details to his standard offerings that reflect a balanced dance with some very real constraints. His preference is for small wood-heated,

Sauna built from another architect's plans that matched it with a ski chalet near Mad River Glen.

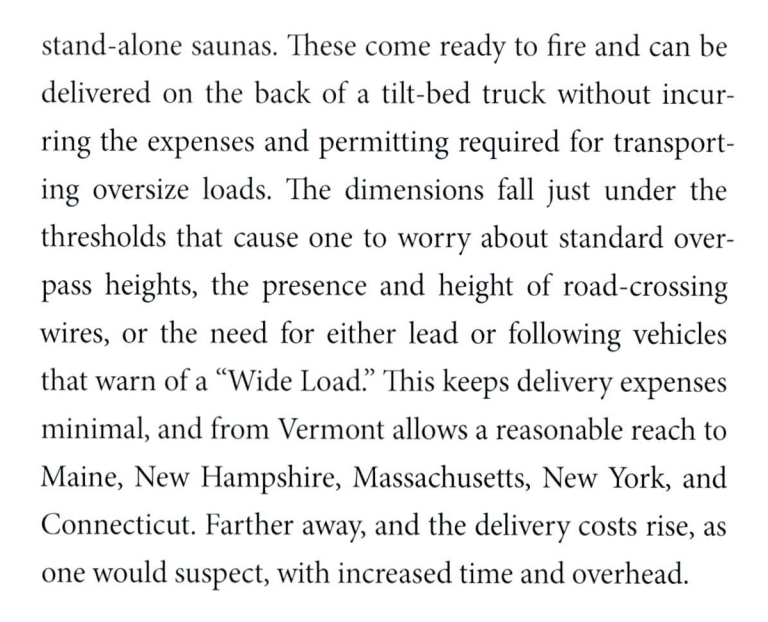

Even when building from plans other than his own, Nils has some signature features, such as clean, simple lines and simple pegs for hanging clothes in the changing/cooling room.

stand-alone saunas. These come ready to fire and can be delivered on the back of a tilt-bed truck without incurring the expenses and permitting required for transporting oversize loads. The dimensions fall just under the thresholds that cause one to worry about standard overpass heights, the presence and height of road-crossing wires, or the need for either lead or following vehicles that warn of a "Wide Load." This keeps delivery expenses minimal, and from Vermont allows a reasonable reach to Maine, New Hampshire, Massachusetts, New York, and Connecticut. Farther away, and the delivery costs rise, as one would suspect, with increased time and overhead.

The other constraint faced by those with an interest in meticulous artistry is that the required time inherent in taking extra care can escalate the cost of a finished product. Nils has been ingenious in the creation of a number of jigs, templates, and techniques that add some speed to the basic building process, which then allows for fussy custom precision to be employed where refinements and details call for it.

In addition to traditional free-standing saunas, Nils is happy to be contracted for designs, building wood, or electric-heated sauna rooms inside homes or other structures, or for building on site either from his own plans or those of other architects. Occasionally he gets to build a log sauna, his favorite and, of course, the real traditional way in Finland.

Because exacting standards have evolved along with his research and empirical observations as a builder, another set of skills has co-evolved—those of persuasive diplomat. Outside the realm of his shop, where autonomous control prevails, is the arena where cooperation among architects, home-owners, and contractor/builder must be gracefully achieved. Occasionally Nils finds himself in the role of facilitator of communication, educator, and gentle bender of wills. There are times when he would prefer to rein in the artistic fancies of an architect or a homeowner's vision of uniqueness if the results stray too far from a builder's practical needs, or unwittingly introduce longer-term problems structurally, or simply overlook flow and convenience within limited space. Most folks respond well to direct expert counsel as offered by Nils. A few he can cajole into accepting the best way forward by presenting cautionary considerations in a manner that allows the recipient to believe such forethought is their own idea. Occasionally he must accept what might be called the "specialists dilemma," bite his tongue, swallow any frustration, proceed with directives as delivered, and refrain from saying "I told you so" when foreseen avoidable issues unfold later.

A tour of his shop revealed a space just big enough for his needs. While I was impressed with a neat, organized space that might have appealed to a Swiss watchmaker, Nils was apologizing for the "mess" as evidenced by a work in progress and the presence of various extension cords snaking here and there to power spot-specific lighting and an array of tools left within easy reach.

As with many craftsmen, Nils regards some aspects of the work as proprietary. While acknowledging that anyone could discern his designs and techniques by visiting him personally or visiting anyone who has his finished work, he asked me not to photograph an elegant window system that was in progress and not yet hidden by trim. A picture taken then would reveal what in effect would be an exploded diagram of the joinery. He didn't want to make it too easy for just anyone to copy such details. While some might find his standards a bit strict and his protectiveness curmudgeonly, the more he explained as we came to know each other the more my appreciation and admiration grew.

There is always more to the equation than the built structure itself. Simple elegance often involves complex thought, and Nils works very much under the premise that value considered infuses the value of a product delivered. His vision starts with siting, how the landscape and approach relate to activity and process. As such he is an ecologist of both the physical and the personal space of sauna. Even in the absence of specific knowledge of an owner's site and the potential for the site to evolve or the building to be moved to a different location, owner, or environment over time, his creations come with a built-in flexibility and grace. Somehow he masters a paradox, simultaneously providing artistic precision in details while retaining gorgeously adaptive simplicity.

The results are a gift delivered to those he builds for. And the dreaming does not stop there. As he builds he is always thinking about means and technique. Occasionally he writes notes, makes sketches, or outlines order for presentation. There are drafts of chapters for a sauna building manual accumulating on his computer. At the moment, time is not readily available for a book project, but the percolation process is under way.

When Nils peruses his extensive library of all things sauna, especially the how-to section, he shakes his head at the many shortcomings he observes in even the best of these publications. He knows he can do better, somehow create a really completely good offering in an accessible friendly language and tone with clear and digestible examples and illustrations. This will come to pass. He speaks shyly and infrequently of these book-writing goals, but radiates excitement and conviction when he does. The drive and desire is fully there; it is just a matter of timing. In the meantime we can all hope that the unfolding is sooner rather than later.

Not long into my first visit Nils fired up his sauna, and two friends arrived to share the firing and supper following. The sauna is slightly smaller than what his current offerings have evolved to, but it held the four of us with space to spare. For two, or as a solo event, it would provide a heavenly stretched-out luxury. Illumination was provided by a gently flickering candle.

Just before entering, I had been looking at the glossy catalogs of some of the larger sauna companies that Nils had in his library. Something about them was unsettling, but I couldn't quite define what. Then after the second cooling session, back in the warm light with the calm, clean lines of shadowed wood enveloping us, a contrasting picture emerged. Nils and his companion were closest to the light source and illuminated enough so I could see they were animated by their quiet conversation. The other guest was sitting cross-legged with the perfect posture of a yoga practitioner on the other end of the bench I shared. Her eyes were closed, and she was dreamily lost within the privacy of sublime relaxation. Only the highlights on cheekbones, shoulders, and knees showed in the subtle light. What finally sifted into my thinking was that some of the sauna companies were evolving away from the traditional close, warm glow toward the bright showroom and glittery end of the spectrum. It reflected a different esthetic that valued what I was coming to regard as over-the-top mood lighting. For me, such effects amounted to visual noise rather than promoting a contemplative and calming ambience.

Embraced by the heat of Nils's sauna, in the comforting glow of a candle and basking in the warmth of new friends, I began to get a vocabulary for tastes and preferences I had intuitively understood and favored but could not have articulated. When Nils reaches into the quiver of lighting options and chooses a candle over the latest in multi-colored fiber optics and LED technology that can be coupled with sound systems and programmed to flash different brightnesses as the music changes, he is not only courting a very much older, more romantic aspect of sauna magic, but inviting us to understand that lighting provides more than the visible spectrum our eyes perceive. He knows that embracing magic involves all the senses, breath and heart, and the tribal glow invoked by flame. Rather than saying so out loud, he would simply invite us to sauna, allowing that given the chance, we might see it that way too. It seems to happen spontaneously when the light is low and quiet and flickers a little.

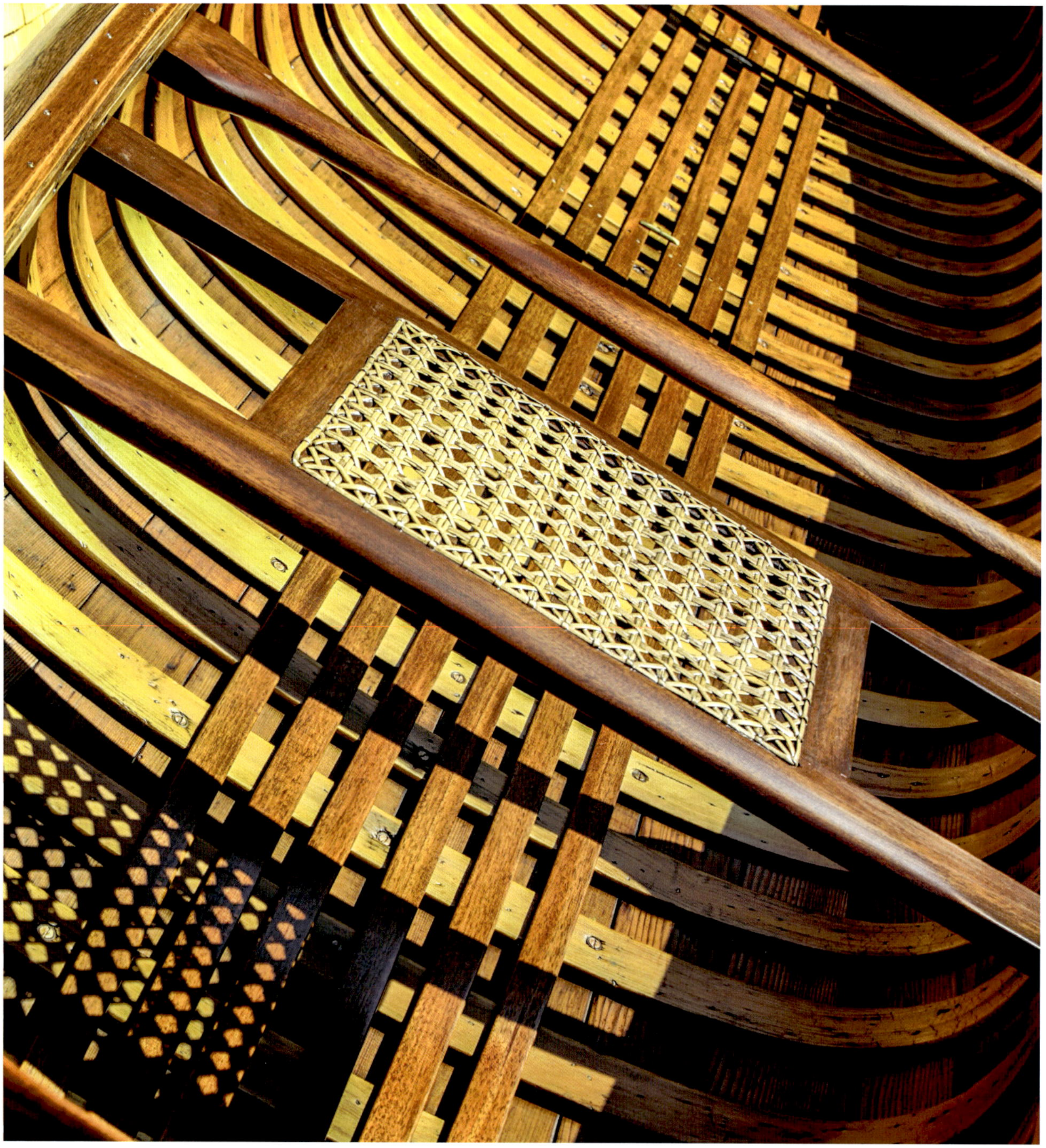

CHAPTER 3

Northwoods Canoe Sauna

Atkinson, Maine, is not the type of place that typically merits a second glance. It is small enough, and spread out enough, that most people passing through wouldn't even discern a "town" to aim a glance at even if they were alert and fast enough to do so. It was historically more populous. There was a sequence of water-driven mills along Alder Stream, the most recent being a shingle mill, although only the foundation stones reveal its presence now. Ninety men were sent to the Civil War. There are a remarkable number of cemeteries for such a tiny place, and it seems that the headstones outnumber the living. Even a coffin factory closed more than a generation ago.

The people who do give it a second glance tend to be those with an eye for hidden charms and a feel for that which does not meet the eye. Conservationist Charles Fitzgerald spent thirty years buying woodlots and abandoned farms in an effort to protect the watershed of Alder Stream. Now those holdings are managed as an ecological reserve by a trio of conservation partners, the Sweetwater Trust, the Northeast Wilderness Trust, and the Forest Society of Maine. A renowned and influential sustainable-yield forester named Mel Ames conducts his exemplary forestry in Atkinson on his home woodlot. An award-winning taxidermist has a studio in town. And two world-class wooden canoe builders keep their shops there.

A visitor might imagine that the town has some strange zoning ordinance that favors obscurity. While these enterprises can be found, and some even have a modest sign, don't expect a series of strategically placed signs to guide you along the rural tributary roads from the nearest numbered routes. The name of Rollin Thurlow's enterprise is the Northwoods Canoe Company. Northwoods, while descriptive, could be anywhere in the circumpolar north: Maine, Canada, Scandinavia, or somewhere in Siberia. Jerry Stelmok of Island Falls Canoe Company builds canoes on century-old forms of the E. M. White Company, which never had a connection to Island Falls. It's just that Jerry never changed the name when he acquired the forms from a previous owner who did have a connection to Island Falls. But then, he's the type of guy who never took the previous homeowner's name off of his mailbox and replaced it with his own, because the local rural carrier knew who he was anyway.

In the case of the two canoe shops, there is an explanation for any deliberate or accidental lack of visibility; both are world famous, and neither would benefit from a local profile. The regional Chamber of Commerce has remained steadfastly unaware of them, and shippers, delivery services, and patrons are given directions as needed. Part of the lore and lure among those who treat a visit to the shops as a pilgrimage is the sense that their quests, travels, and setbacks share the literary elements that make up the heroes' journey of classic mythology. Even in the age of Google Earth, GPS, and in-vehicle computers, shipping container, UPS, and Fed EX drivers show a trace of pride upon arrival after successfully traversing the roads where low spots with spotty connectivity are prevalent and ridge tops with reception few and far between.

The Wooden Boat School regards Jerry and Rollin as the Alpha and Omega of the wooden canoe world. They have earned their place at the highest end of the spectrum by producing an inspiring stream of classic canoes, books, instructional videos, and works of art. They co-authored *The Wood and Canvas Canoe*, which is the shop manual and dreamer's text for anyone and everyone with an interest in the historic and contemporary world of wooden canoes. Both live in Atkinson. Both enjoy sauna.

Jerry's came with his current home; it's a small family sauna snuggled like a large closet next to the main chimney that accepts its stove pipe. Rollin's was made later as an addition to the home and shop complex he designed and built himself.

Rollin and Andrea were the most ardent regulars at my own sauna on the Wilson Stream. They rarely missed any opportunities when a firing was announced, despite a forty-minute drive to partake. I happened to be present when Andrea decided that what she wanted for her combined sixtieth birthday and retirement from teaching was her own sauna. Rollin observed this request with his usual amusing slant: "But I'm male, I've never even heard of birthdays unless I thought I could get some cake and ice cream out of one. This only gives me a couple of years to comply.…"

"I know. That's why I told you now."

You needed to be present to feel how sweetly such a truth was told. And to see Rollin's eyes light up as his imagination began to run with the idea. Andrea is generous, caring sweetness personified. Any of us within the sphere of her radiance would do anything for her, like willing Chevaliers eager for the approval of a benevolent queen. And while Rollin can be pretty good at projecting a bristly curmudgeonly persona, he's a warm softy underneath the bluff and bluster.

Andrea at the doorway of her combined retirement and birthday gift.

In a far corner of the paint room in the canoe shop is Rollin's drafting table. It is affixed to hinges and folds down from the wall so it doesn't take up space that is usually crowded with canoes resplendent in their bright finishes. When there are no fresh paint or varnish fumes thickening the air he can put some music on, wend his way back there, flip the table down, and concentrate on anything from the finer points of architecture for a building to the lines to transfer to a lofting bed for a boat design.

Craftsmanship of the sort Rollin engages with combines simultaneous attention to fine detail and the big picture. He tends not just to the physical presence of a project, but to context, history, tradition, and artistry. Everything that might come to bear gets considered.

Fold-down drafting table at the back of the paint room in the canoe shop.

He built his house wide and it faces south to maximize passive solar gain. It is relatively shallow in depth, the better to receive the reach of radiance and light. It is set into a slope to maximize gain from earth heat. Any expansion potential tends to be northward, which is the shady and least-acknowledged side. When the canoe company office had to grow, the extension emerged from the north wall. A sauna could fit back there, but where? It had to fold into existing shape and function sensibly and well.

The office created a bit of an ell to the back wall, and Rollin thought that an extension of his bedroom the same length as the office would make it possible to blend the necessary additional roof extension into a single edge the full width of the back. Since the bedroom was at the far end from the office, there would be an empty span between the two. A sauna in the corner made by the bedroom would tuck things together nicely. That still left a short gap to the edge of the office, perfect for a sauna entry zone on one side and a wood pile backed against the office wall on the other. The single common roof edge would cover all and shelter the woodpile and sauna entry. He kept that space open to the woods in back.

A doorway added to the back wall of Andrea's office, which is just off the kitchen/living room space, would provide seamless access to the sauna and wood storage area beyond. The wooded back yard would allow

Boat builder's esthetics reflected in the top bench of the Northwoods Canoe Sauna.

Slate and brick heat shields surround the stove.

complete privacy for cooling off between sauna sessions in the open air of the entry area.

At some point, Rollin must have leaned back from the drafting table with a satisfied grin. Simple lines, maximum gain, and easy flow patterns between rooms and outside. Better yet, getting wood to the living room stove would no longer require a climb from the cellar, but would come direct from the wood piles in back without change of elevation or a circuitous route involving multiple corners and stairs.

There was only one problem. Despite a couple of years of lead time before Andrea's combined birthday and retirement celebration, Rollin was many years into the maximum level of shop operation with no relief in sight. His work falls neatly into thirds. One-third of his business is new canoes, one third is restorations, and one third is a mail-order component for hard-to-find, often obscure marine fittings, specialized tools, and fastenings peculiar to the world of wooden canoes. Despite having a full-time partner in the shop and a part-time person who combines the roles of office manager, shipping-room person, and communications/billing person, customers have an eighteen- to twenty-four-month wait period between a canoe order and delivery. He needed time and didn't have it.

But then, one of the niceties of rural living in an area with limited "real" jobs is that there are lots of entrepreneurs who are skilled tradesmen. Rollin easily found someone to prepare the site and pour concrete. Another friend had the skills and was eager to take on the framing and finish work of roof extension, bedroom extension, and building of the sauna. Work in the shop would remain uninterrupted, and Dave Bessler, "ace carpenter" as he calls himself, had a project that intrigued him. Andrea's celebratory deadline had the appearance of being a comfortably long way off. Although Rollin was twenty years into his career before he managed to build himself one of his own superb wilderness canoes, the completion of Andrea's sauna wishes came true a little ahead of schedule. She hadn't yet reached the target birthday and retirement was likewise an anticipated event some months in the future when the first firing took place.

Rollin once told a journalist: "Behind every successful boat builder is a spouse with a job and a health plan." Now it seemed a good time to ask Andrea about her side of the equation. Maybe behind one particular smiling sauna owner is a funny, ironic, competent, and sometimes curmudgeonly sweetheart canoe builder that can get things done.

Rollin firing up.

Delight in the heat.

Cooling pool with sauna (banya in Russian), combined with a shop and garage.

CHAPTER 4

Community Sauna in East Blue Hill

The glaciers that sculpted the Maine coast from Brunswick eastward to Lubec and Eastport created a convoluted interface between land and sea that is complex and beautiful. Depending on one's mood or need to hurry, such a place can be endearingly inconvenient or completely exasperating for anyone trying to get from one place to another. The granitic ribs of bedrock that resisted the ice tend to be oriented north and south. Most of these ribs are long and narrow with corresponding long, narrow bays separating them. Offshore, everything remains as complicated as the adjacent land. These are island-studded waters, and while the generally north-south dimensions of the islands stay consistent with the landscape features, there is much to bewilder the navigator. Only winged creatures experience any opportunity for directness between where they are and a destination. To keep things interesting for anyone engaged with this land and seascape, the winds, tides, currents, fog, rain squalls, and snow storms provide all sorts of occasionally lethal variables to remind everyone not to become complacent. People who can see an adjacent town a short distance across the water may need to travel multiples of that distance to get there by land. Island dwellers arrange their lives around ferry schedules. While on the water, mariners need to be versed in all the variables a twelve-foot tide can introduce in the forms of currents, reversing rapids, and the presence or absence of ragged, menacing ledges. Circuitous passage among islands, across bays, and around the countless intrusions of mainland peninsulas is ever the norm, while single reach line-of-sight navigation remains an unusual opportunity.

A place of strong physical character tends to attract inhabitants who are characters themselves. Listen to any of the songs and stories that arise from coastal Maine and you soon fall under a spell of wry ironic humor, indirectness, telling details, and diversions that convey essential information, but often for reasons not immediately apparent. Circumlocutions of speech mirror the circumnavigation requirements of passage upon land and water. My eventual arrival at Sergei and Katya's sauna was appropriately indirect despite being able to get there on mainland roads.

In 1989, the year the Iron Curtain fell, Sergei Breus left St. Petersburg, Russia, and eventually found his way to Surry, Maine. An oceanographer and teacher in his homeland, he put his builder's skills front and foremost once in Maine and has been building stunningly gorgeous houses in the mid-coast region for some time now. His own magnificent house provides an example, as does a replica, on an adjacent lot, of Russian poet Aleksandr Pushkin's *dacha*, complete with the traditional Russian tamarack roof covering of edge-butted boards running vertically from crest to eave. Katya arrived later, and she and Sergei have a sweet five-year-old bilingual daughter named Anya. Katya's mother, also Anya, is a gentle, handsome woman who shares the household and has taken it upon herself to keep the vegetable gardens and ornamentals of the grounds well cared for. For young Anya, the presence of her babushka organically favors all the benefits of extended family, second-language fluency beyond her parents and ties to the country of her heritage.

Sergei grew up within the tradition of *banya*, the Russian equivalent of sauna, and the older form *porchenomo*, or "in black," which corresponds to the *savusauna* or smoke sauna in Finland. The smoke sauna involves the heating of a huge mass of rocks inside the structure, but without benefit of a chimney or an enclosed stove and stovepipe. The room itself fills with hot smoke, which is vented until totally replaced with fresh air after the fire is allowed to burn out. At that time, any embers and burning matter are cleaned from the hearth, and the ferociously hot rocks heat the refreshed air. The pile of rocks takes a good portion of the day to heat, but holds that intense heat for nearly a full day afterwards. The walls and benches darken over time from the smoke. Those who have experienced smoke sauna are enthusiastically adamant that the quality of the heat cannot be matched or even approximated by a stove-heated sauna. It is both deeper and "softer," and the scent of the fire itself infusing the room adds another dimension.

When Sergei first arrived in Maine, he became friends with many of the people involved with the Maine Organic Farmers and Gardeners Association (MOFGA), who had in turn been supremely influenced by Helen and Scott Nearing, the authors of *Living the Good Life*. By accident of timing, the book galvanized a generation of seekers looking to make sense of the fertile cauldron of change that emerged for those coming of age in the 1960s. As articulate spokespeople for an alternative social order based on healthy and choiceful living that merged seamlessly with the back-to-the land movement, the Nearings found themselves catapulted into the role of patron saints of one of the waves of utopian thinking that periodically surge through our collective consciousness. The difference with the wave at the cusp of the

1970s was that it was not just another recurring trend, but like Thoreau's *Walden*, became a groundswell of tsunami proportions and proved to have lasting impact far beyond the specifics of its vision.

Not surprisingly, a cluster of the most serious of the Nearings' protégés settled near Harborside on Cape Rosier, adjacent to the Nearings' farm, where many continue to be among the primary practitioners and advocates of sustainable organic agriculture. Eliot Coleman, one of the better-known disciples, had a Finnish-style sauna that hosted a regular community Sunday event. Others soon built saunas, and a Wednesday night sauna and supper tradition that would rotate among the different farmsteads evolved. Whether by accident or design, the Cape Rosier Good Lifers mirrored the Finnish tradition of a mid-week and weekend sauna. Sergei, fresh from the *banya* traditions of his home country, was delighted to find and be folded into a thriving sauna culture springing up on a mid-coast peninsula in Maine.

Six years ago, Sergei built his own *banya* in East Blue Hill. He refers to it as a sauna, the more familiar term among Americans, and, as often happens, his too has had a glorious impact upon the neighborhood and greater community.

My own visit came about as the result of circuitous serendipity. Someone who lives 80 miles from East Blue Hill as a peregrine falcon might fly but 130 miles by road happened to tell me of a glorious sauna owned by a Russian couple I would simply "have to meet." A year and a half earlier, another person had told me her next door neighbors had a beautiful sauna, and she would see if I could visit sometime. It turned out each of these people were talking about the same sauna, and that they also knew each other. Through one of them I got the address of the owners, but initial correspondence was not immediately answered. Instead, a welcoming invitation filtered through each of the friends some time later.

The intrigue continued. Lucy and her husband Clifton hosted me, but directions to Lucy's had come via the other friend. Sergei was still mysterious, although he drove by and was pointed out by Clifton after I arrived. Clifton had lit the sauna in a timely manner, but would not be joining the festivities. A swarm of kids charged around outside, delighting in that part of spring where the snow has suddenly vanished. Occasionally, they dashed into the house for some water or an apple. Some of them were Lucy and Clifton's, some not. Shimmering heat waves without smoke exited the stovepipe of the sauna next door, indicating that the fire was burning at full combustion and probably had been for some time. It was likely that the room was ready, although no one specifically said it was time to go. Nevertheless, an unspoken gravitational force was at play, and Lucy and I drifted over with our contributions to the potluck supper to follow sauna.

Sunday Sauna in East Blue Hill is a community event, frequent enough so that it is assumed to be "on" unless otherwise noted. Few communications are necessary for Sergei and Katya to let word circulate among the regulars when it is not going to occur should they be too busy or absent. Such would be the case for the following Sunday, when they would be traveling to Boston for a Russian Easter service.

The sauna is incorporated into the northwest corner of a larger structure. Even with the stovepipe visible there is nothing of outward appearances to suggest a lovely sauna is housed within. An observer on the road below might simply assume that a shop, apartment, or studio was combined with a garage. A gorgeous house with a red roof perches a short distance beyond, with an expanse of tall windows favoring a view of the bay and catching maximum sun.

A man ascending the driveway with a red balloon tethered by a ribbon greeted Lucy and me as we approached the house cross-lots. He explained he had just come from his daughter's fourth birthday party. The daughter soon scampered into view and took my hand to ease her up a set of adult-sized cut granite steps. Inside I met Sergei and a few others, and said hello to a cluster of kids engaged with a game of Uno. Sergei is a beaming man who radiates infinite charm. "Please, head down, it's ready," he said, and the balloon-toting dad and I eagerly headed toward the sauna.

The instant we opened the changing-room door we were greeted by the welcoming hot, dry scent of a sauna seasoned to temperature. After introducing ourselves to each other as we disrobed, we entered the hot room quickly and together to minimize any cooler air coming in with us. A woman in a colorful sari-like wrap was already blissfully there--she had been there long enough to be shiny-eyed and radiant with the heat. She and I shook hands and exchanged names as I passed to an upper bench, and she addressed the other man by name, being already familiar. While my companions traded neighborly news, I had time to feast my eyes on the details of the room.

A window centered in the west wall and another in the north wall filled the room with late afternoon light. Although not yet needed, an electric red light was on to provide illumination after dark, the advantage being that the wavelength of red light does not diminish one's night vision when passing from sauna to subtly lit changing room to outside dark. The stove was fed from the changing room, and was set low within the hot room and nearly invisible beneath a crown of sauna stones. It was a regular cast iron stove for space heating, but Sergei had created a fire-safe shielded passage through the wall, despite it not being a sauna stove manufactured with a collar for that purpose. Without a built-in cradle to hold them, the stones were simply heaped on the flat surface, and that limited area was expanded by a matrix of

Jessica, one of the Sunday firing regulars, emerges from the cooling pool like a sylvan goddess.

iron bars spanning a low brick wall that boxed in the stove. The brickwork separated the stove from the adjacent entryway and provided a heat shield to the corner behind it. In addition, the bricks deflected the heat upward, maximizing convection, and prevented a direct blast from making the closest bench across the entryway too hot. The stovepipe had another, larger, diameter pipe section around it, creating an inch or two of airspace between the two. This configuration also favored convection while preventing the pipe heat from blasting directly onto anyone on the bench that ended just shy of the stove.

Wide low benches and slightly narrower top benches were along the side and back walls. Only a short walkway extended from the changing room door into the room, stepped near the back for easier access to the top benches. Benches on the side occupied by the stove were shorter by just enough to preserve safe distancing for both framing and the comfort of bathers. All benches received good heat. The low ones were slightly above the height of the stove and stones, and the high benches were well above that. A flat ceiling kept the heat close for maximum intensity. Two carved ladles, a tall wooden bucket filled with heated water, and two bundles of leafy red oak twigs sat on the low bench closest to the stove.

During the ebb and flow of conversation, Lucy arrived, as did Sergei and two others. The first woman bade us goodbye and departed just as someone else arrived. It turned out that they were the parents of the Uno players inside, and this "changing of the guard" was the shift-point between forty-five-minute sessions of child supervision while the other enjoyed forty-five minutes of unfettered child-free sauna time.

In the cozy communal embrace of the room, friends and friends of friends were equally welcome, and newcomers elicited no surprise. All were folded into any conversations punctuating sequences of quiet basking. An easy flow of happy revelers came and went as each settled into a personal pace for heating and cooling and as early arrivals departed and later visitors arrived. As many as eight or ten might occupy the benches at any one time, occasionally dwindling to just one or two, allowing a few quiet moments of lull while most were outside cooling.

A woman in a light robe with her hair tucked under a felt sauna cap entered. Katya. At some point, more wood was added to the stove to keep the heat hovering at 200 degrees or a little above. As we responded to our differing cooling needs, the increased traffic through the entry introduced cooler air, but this was countered by attentive stove keeping.

Outside there were benches along the wall for those wishing to air-cool. An outdoor shower emerged from the same wall, but the pipes would remain drained until later in the season, when the possibility of freezing no longer threatened. Directly in line with the changing-room door, a set of cut granite steps ascended a bank and similarly descended into a small dug pond created as an artful center to the sauna setting. Earlier in the day, Sergei had cut away an accommodating rectangle of ice with a chainsaw, and we now had access to the water for more radical cooling. It seemed all of us used the opportunity at least once, while several found a dip in the pond appealing for all cooling sessions.

Ever the genial host, Sergei offered Katya and each guest a lovely session with the oak whisks. While I had experienced using birch whisks in several saunas, and had reciprocated whisking the backs of adjacent bench-mates, this had always been done while sitting. In the East Blue Hill sauna, this delicious nicety was more stylized and elaborate.

The person ready to be whisked would stretch out face down on the top bench with forearms crossed and cradling their head. Sergei inserted a rolled towel beneath the insteps to allow the feet to be supported at a comfortable angle rather than flattened on the bench. The whisks were taken from their warm water soak in the bucket and shaken over the stones to release a powerful burst of oak scented steam. He then assumed a stance reminiscent of a dramatic kettle drum player in an orchestra, and waved the whisks like ceiling fans above the person relaxed on the bench, driving the hottest air at ceiling level downward. After a few seconds of being certain that the person below was engulfed by luscious heat he began a gentle whisking from the backs of the arms above the head, across the neck and shoulders and on down the entire back side and each leg, finishing with attention to the soles of the feet.

Then he started again at the arms, neck, and shoulders, continuing all the way to the feet and arches. This time the whisking was a little harder, and the rhythm and rustling of the whisks enhanced the stimulation to the skin, while the leafy scent of hot oak infused the room to the pleasure of all. Following this, Sergei held both bundles in one hand and pressed with the other while giving a firm continuous leafy scrub from shoulder all the way down to the feet—one gently abrasive full length swipe on each side of the spine.

Again the bundles were dipped into the bucket and rinsed, and the stones sprinkled. Another whirling of the whisks like fans above would be followed by an even more vigorous full length whisking and rub down.

Sergei's offer was gratefully accepted by all of us remaining. When it was my turn I simply couldn't believe how transcendent and remarkable each aspect was. Indeed, I could hardly move immediately afterwards, as if to do so would diminish such overwhelming goodness. Best of all my legs still tingled nearly full length from the final leafy whisking on the arches of my feet, sending shivers akin to mild electricity upward well past my knees.

When the person getting whisked lay on their back to receive the leafy stimulation on their front side, women shielded their breasts with their hands, and men would likewise cover their sensitive parts, allowing the full brisk treatment to continue without interruption or reduced effect.

Afterwards, in the descending dusk, while walking up toward the house I resolved to offer to whisk Sergei next time I might be lucky enough to visit. It seemed in the sequence of events that he had been completely generous, but not a receiver of such a treat. I was happy to learn later that Katya had reciprocated while I was engaged in conversation while cooling outside.

In the kitchen, just before settling in to the pleasures of continued conversation and a splendid meal, Sergei poured each of us a shot of super-chilled vodka. Even the shot glasses had been chilled and were frosty. My first attempt at a proper single-gulp Russian toast resulted in an embarrassing tentative sip, but a silver-haired gentleman named Mark noticed and offered coaching. "Let's try that again," he said. "It's okay because it is so chilled. Smooth and good, you'll see." He added, "Also, you must make serious direct eye contact with the person you are making the toast with. This is ceremonial, a pact of trust and friendship." He enjoyed a second shot via the teaching, and, emboldened by his confidence-building care, I achieved success. It was smooth, pure, crisp, and a total delight, followed by an involuntary appreciative gasp much like one might make observing a particularly rewarding burst of northern lights in an already spectacular display. Sergei grinned, and ushered us all toward the dining table with a magnanimous sweep of his arm.

Sergei, still aglow from the heat, shares a properly chilled vodka toast with a guest.

Sergei, slicing organic beef and pork he raised himself, as part of the potluck to follow a Sunday firing.

Bill framed by both the exterior door to the changing room and the door to the hot room.

58

CHAPTER 5

Details Closely Honed

But for a zig and a retreating zag in the boundary where a triangle of Lamoille County intrudes into Caledonia County, Bill Morrison's place would be in Vermont's Northeast Kingdom. Psychologically and by habitat it is, and I prefer to mentally straighten the boundary so that the town of Wolcott, Bill's homestead, Tamarack Brook, and Bear Swamp fall fictitiously on the Caledonia side of the line.

Northeast Kingdom contains the best of the ragged edges of Vermont. The Kingdom itself is somewhat fictitious. You won't find it marked anywhere cartographically; you just have to know that it includes Caledonia, Orleans, and Essex Counties, and tucks itself into the corner that shares a border with Quebec and the northern reaches of New Hampshire. There are plenty of farms and domesticated landscapes, but the forest type leans toward higher latitudes. Hardwoods are still dominant, but the spruce and fir of the boreal regions have a significant presence. Better yet, there are extensive bogs where black spruce and tamarack hint of a wilder north. Dr. Steve Young founded the Center for Northern Studies in Wolcott, near Bear Swamp, in part because of its northern appeal. Students from all over the world would find their way there to pursue studies and research within the realms of science, resource issues, and occasionally politics of the circumpolar north. Renowned naturalists, scientists, ethnographers, and folklorists would quietly filter in and out of the center with the same discrete lack of fanfare that black-backed woodpeckers, boreal chickadees, and Canada jays might occupy the island of northness in Bear Swamp, ever so far south of where you'd expect them.

Poet David Budbill of *Judevine* fame and novelist Howard Frank Mosher were denizens of the Kingdom. For twenty-five years, Sterling College in Craftsbury Common hosted the Wildbranch Writers Workshop. Anyone who delights in a region protected by bad roads and a lack of big towns finds the place appealing. In 2002, after twenty-nine years of teaching genetics and biology at Shippensburg University in Pennsylvania, Bill Morrison was able to retire to a lovely place at the end of a slim dirt road just a stone's throw from Bear Swamp. How

Bill Morrison sauna, Vermont.

he found the location I don't know. But upon meeting, we discovered we were both alumni of the Wildbranch Workshop, and knew a great many people in common.

Kati Osgood, who has been my source of all things Finnish and sauna-related, not to mention a great additional mix of other interests over several decades, was the one who made the connection to Bill. "You have to visit Bill," she said. "His is the most beautiful sauna I have seen this side of the Atlantic."

April was unfolding when our respective schedules favored a meeting. Hooded mergansers were already arriving and occupying the first hints of open water in the still ice-clad ponds and lakes. Early arriving kestrels were perched on road edge wires, ever-patient for mice scurrying in the now snow-free fields below. Sugaring season was well under way in the thick of warm days and nights that obligingly dipped below freezing. The dirt county roads were living up to the legendary glories of mud season. One minute you would be slithering and fishtailing in structureless, slick mud where the sun had beat the frost from the road, and the next you would be cross-threaded in iron-hard frozen ruts where the cold-keeping shadows of evergreen trees crossed the road or the slope of the land pitched the surface away from the direct gaze of the sun. Those encounters never lacked drama, with every loose item in the vehicle rattling like a cyclone and the teeth in your skull chipping and chattering against each other. At the end of a public town road, a transition occurred and Bill's private drive continued on to a beautiful post-and-beam house above a small pond that has a sauna perched at its edge.

Bill greeted me and over lunch we could scarcely keep our eclectic interests from running away with our attentions. But Kati would be joining us soon, and another friend, John, was due to arrive. Before firing up, there were some things Bill wanted to show me.

One side of Bill's family heritage is Lithuanian. He had a scrapbook of some visits there, and it included several shots of the Lithuanian equivalent of sauna, known as *pirtis*. Unlike Finnish saunas, which usually favor a low-angle roof, the Lithuanian tradition seemed to prefer a rather tall steep roof; I had noticed that Bill's had this feature as I drove up around the pond. This esthetic is likely a hold-over from when roofs were thatched and steepness maximized water shedding abilities. He explained the term *pirtis* is derived from a root word meaning "to heat," and that the birch twig whisks known as *vihta* or *vasta* in Finnish are called *vanta* in Lithuanian. In the file folder that contained everything related to the building of his sauna, he showed me sketches notated in Lithuanian that had been drawn for him.

Bill's house perches high on a sloped exposure that looks down and over a small pond made deeper by an earth dam that his driveway crosses. The sauna is footed upon large rocks a few feet back from the water's edge. Kati's assessment of compelling beauty had been, if

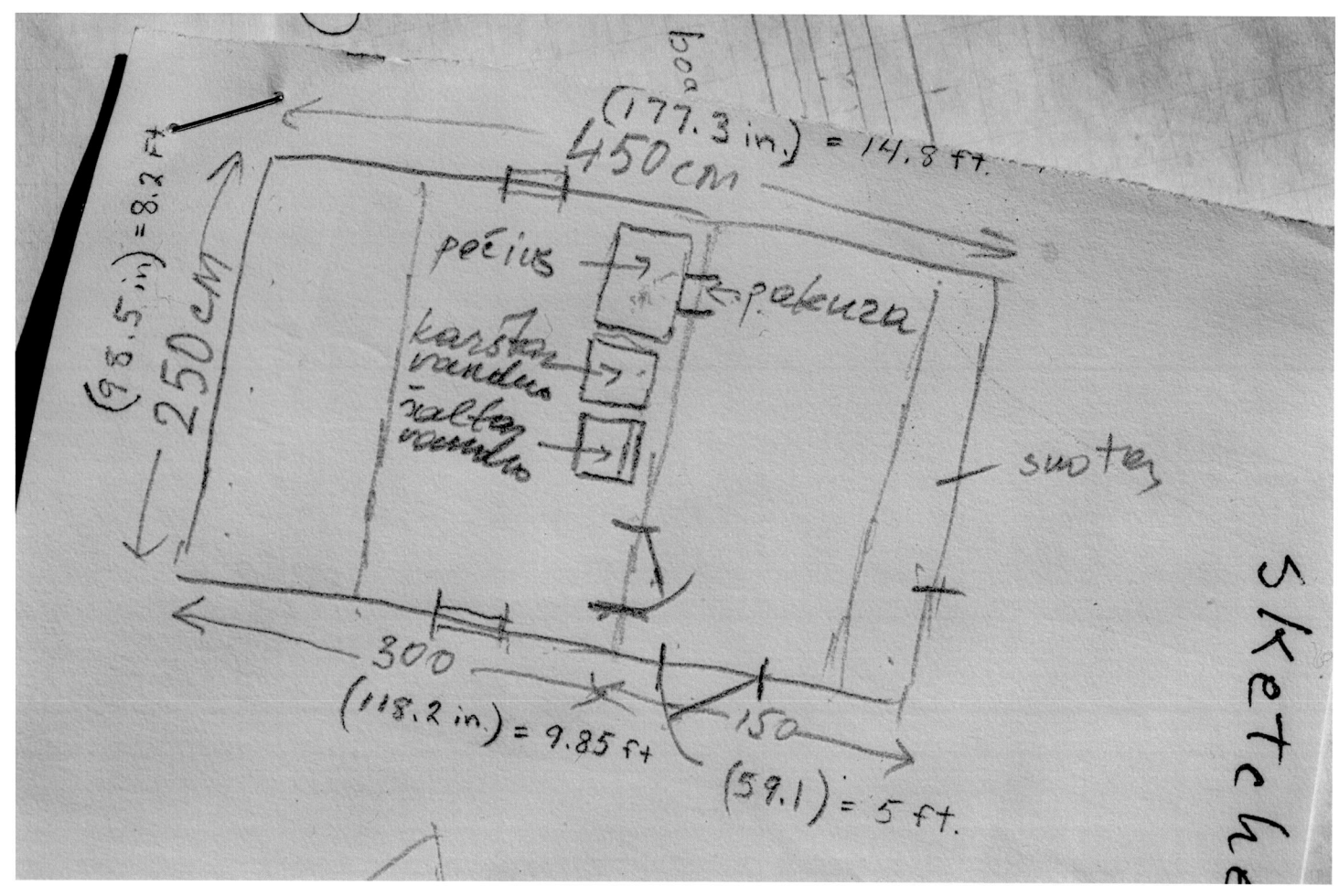

Planning sketches for Bill's sauna, or pirtis in Lithuanian.

anything, a full-fledged Yankee understatement. What Bill has achieved in his site considerations and selective care envelops a visitor with an immediate sense of exquisite calm and balance.

Soon enough we strolled down with a big container of drinking water to get the fire going and everything ready. Even while preoccupied with our preparations, I could see that the sauna was not only well-made with a great deal of care, but done with very close attention to detail and with consummate attention to aspect within the surroundings. "A fella named Luke Hardt built this. I invited him today but he couldn't make it," Bill said. The sauna was a tidy two-room gem with board-and-batten siding, cedar shingles in the gable end, and a crisp steel roof.

"This is stunningly fantastic; I would like to meet him."

With water transferred to buckets and drinking vessels and the fire crackling, Bill ushered me outside, away from the finer details of the builder's artistry. He wanted to start his introductions with the pond and the exposure. Although the near end of the pond couldn't escape the manmade arc of the earthen berm, its farther reaches were very natural looking and reflected an original wetland within the brook, which the dam deepened and expanded in creating the pond. There were cattails and marsh grass in a narrow band before the woods rose around the edges. A big broken-topped white pine was right across, which Bill liked. He excitedly told me it had provided a roost for an arctic-bound rough-legged hawk during migration one spring.

"I wanted Luke to position the sauna so that it lined up with the house, but fortunately he over-ruled me. See how this is just askew? It favors the pond better. When we go inside, if you look out both doors you'll see that the dock aims straight toward that big rock over there. In summer we swim to that to cool off, and it slopes slightly toward the sun, so it is warm to lie on." Back inside I sighted along the perfectly plumb door edges out along the dock, and beyond to the big rock near the far shore. The dock edge was precisely parallel to, and centered on, that line. No details were too small to not be considered, and this of course made big-picture sense. Bill is a detail man. His research at Penn State had to do with tracing the genetics of an enzyme system in trout. The "systems" for the sauna were approached with the same attentiveness. The builder's principles of true, plumb, and level were not something to trifle with, nor were the finer points regarding positioning and placement of the sauna within the greater environment and its specific site.

We walked out on the ice to look back at everything from the pond. The sauna was set among a few lovely white pines, with huge flat flagstones from a local quarry stabilizing the pond edge and acting as a deck in front and along one side of the structure. Only a couple of feet separated the front wall from the pond edge, and the dock projected out far enough so that a full six feet of water was beneath the swim ladder. The steep roof had its own appealing esthetic and was mirrored by a window-filled gable end on the house up the rise beyond. Had Bill not pointed out the few degrees of difference in alignment between house and sauna I doubt I would have noticed a discrepancy.

A narrow dressing room with two large windows facing the pond was just inside the door, which was on the side wall rather than the end. Putting a door under the drip edge was worth the pond-favoring window placement on the end wall as well as perfectly balancing a more convenient approach from the house up the hill and access to the dock into the pond. If it were ever regarded as an issue during rain, it would be simple to install a gutter along the eave to divert any shower of rain-flow cascading off the roof.

At the far end of the changing room was an attractive wood box positioned perfectly for the stove door, which had a through-the-wall extension so that wood never went into the sauna room itself. Stoves with this feature eliminate wasting sauna space with firewood storage, simplify keeping the hot room clean by dispensing with the need to sweep up bark and detritus from wood handling, and the stove not only heats the sauna, but warms the dressing room in the cold seasons when it matters.

The tall roof did not waste space because the framing for the ceiling to retain heat in the sauna room below provided a place to nail floorboards for a storage loft above. The whole front edge of the loft was accessible from the dressing room, which remained open to the roof boards. A window into the sauna room was just above the stove and in line with the dressing room windows so that any daytime sauna use had plenty of natural light as reflected from the pond and the sky above it. Another window was in the wall facing the

An elegant wood box in cooling/changing room adjacent to through-the-wall stove door.

clearing below the house. Both windows had an outside hook to hang a lantern from for illuminating the interior after dark. From the top bench, the side window framed a pleasing view of the farthest reach of the pond.

Inside the sauna room, a concrete floor with a drain sat below a series of duckboard floor components. The duckboards could be removed for periodic cleaning, were warm on bathers' feet, and allowed any water to drain through their spaces to where the floor drain could eliminate any rinse water from bathing and hair washing, or from the swabbing of walls and benches after each sauna.

The room itself was wider than it was long, and benches occupied only the rear wall, the top bench luxuriously wide. The compact layout was pleasing to behold and heated very quickly. The stove had a small glass window so that bathers would be soothed by the flickering of flames.

Kati arrived, and minutes later John pulled in. After greetings and introductions, Bill sent me back down to check the thermometer. His likes a sauna at 180 degrees, and prefers a lot of short sessions of heating and cooling. Back at the house, everyone was happily conversing when I reported that things would be ready in about ten or fifteen minutes.

It seemed all of us shared a sort of boundless interest and enthusiasm for just about everything. A conversation that started out revolving around Bill's collection of German clocks had somehow made an inexplicable leap to the Finnish *kantele*, a simple stringed instrument tuned to a pentatonic scale. Used originally as back-up to the reciting of long stories and poems, they have since come to be played more intricately and often show up among folk musicians with a penchant for reviving interesting ethnic traditions and incorporating them into contemporary acoustics. This allowed Bill to leap up and retrieve a *kantele* he had made and Kati to sing something for which it was perfect accompaniment. Our estimate of minutes passed and we headed to the sauna, but not before Bill got to leap up again to fetch a book he had on something that had arisen as a topic following Kati's song.

Serendipitously, the thermometer was at exactly 180 degrees when we had shed our clothes and entered the sauna. As the afternoon progressed the sun began to favor the side window, confirming the wisdom of the choice to add it to that wall. Inspired by the shifting light, John mentioned that he hoped I could visit his sauna at some point, as his has a stained-glass window he was certain I would appreciate.

After the final cooling there was still a lovely twilight over the pond, and we lingered on the ice, reluctant to leave the spell of eventide. Eventually we headed up to the house for some delicately smoked fish, dark bread, and crackers. This being Cabot Creamery

John, Kati, and Bill enjoying the bench.

After-sauna treats.

country, we also had some "seriously sharp" cheddar cheese. Kati contributed some wondrous organic sausage from a farm just up the road from her home in Northfield, and before we knew it another cascade of topics whirled our conversation in all directions. Only the chiming of German clocks prevented us from lingering into lateness, and we reluctantly expressed our goodnights within a chorus of glowing thanks that had blossomed among new friends.

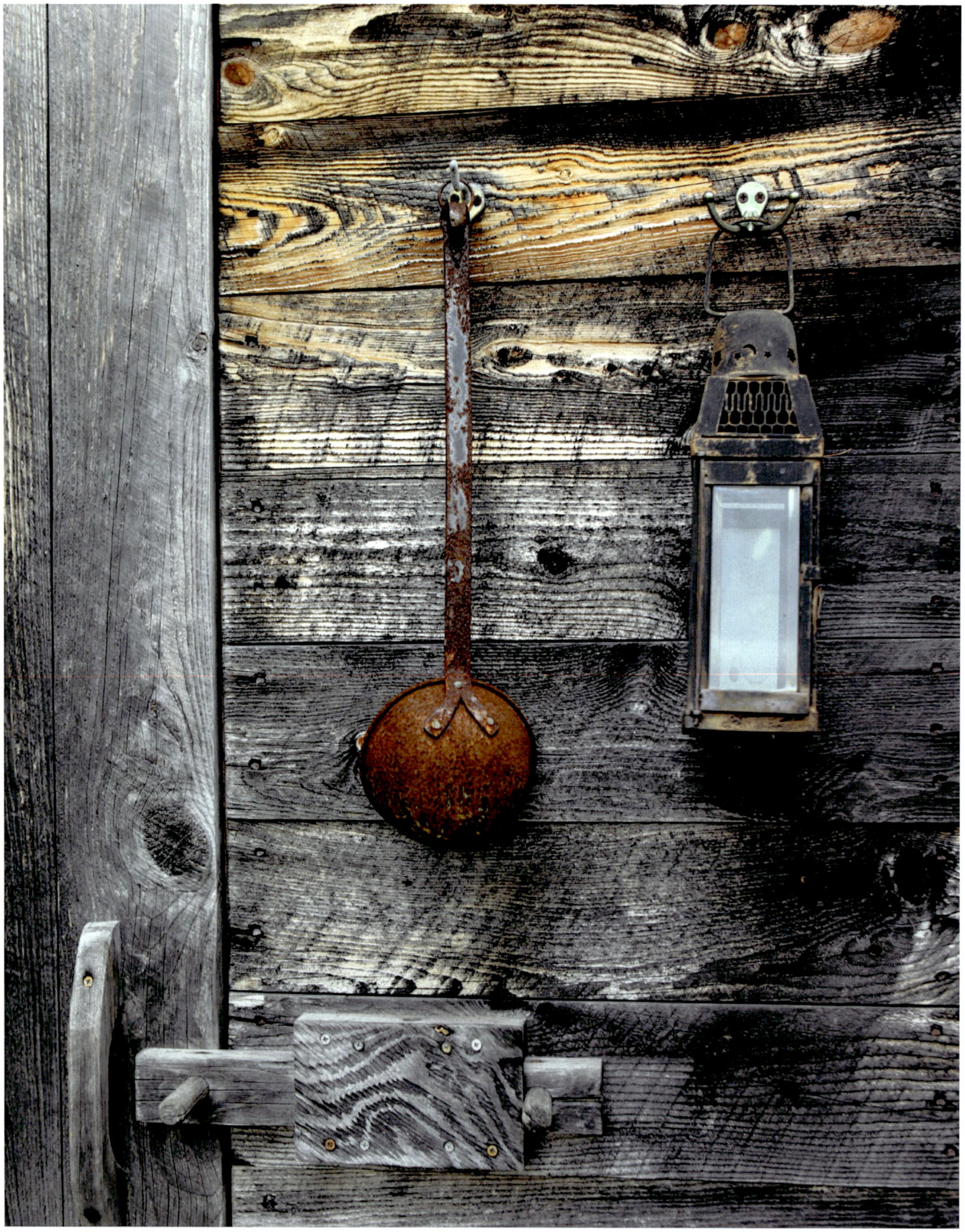

CHAPTER 6

Metamorphosis

The trajectory Mary Flemming took to settle in Moretown, Vermont, has nothing in common with the arc of an archer's arrow. It is a path with plenty of angles, bounce points, and diversions. Some things involved happenstance, but mostly the route was determined by primary interests of the moment. She was born on Cape Breton Island, Nova Scotia; moved to New Brunswick, then to Montreal; attended nursing school in Toronto; then jumped across the border to New Orleans,. then Mississippi, and then Boston. More than twenty years ago she and her partner, Doyle, moved to Vermont in search of "real" winters. After all this time there is still a trace of the Canadian Maritimes' long *o* in a lot of words that other accents construe as an "ow" sound. None of the various accents that are part of her wide-ranging trail have gained a hold in her quiet voice.

Soon after arrival at the Vermont homestead, Doyle built a chicken coop. The chickens seem to have been a presence when the children were very young, but that was some time ago. Both chickens and Doyle have moved on to other things. Yet those times, and fresh eggs, are remembered fondly whenever the kids revisit the homestead and report on their adult dreams and expanding lives. Over time, Mary's house has grown into a cozy place where the rooms and their contents seem to reflect the chambers of an interesting heart. Books are everywhere, and heat from a central stove coils upward through a cathedral-like space where a spiral stair ascends to the upper floor. There are some additions that blend well with the original post-and-beam structure. In front of all, two huge spruce "century trees" planted at the time of the house-raising reach solidly toward the sky. In Mary's world, these are part of the house and render the roof permeable so her senses have access to immediate surroundings or, within the swirl of more expansive moods, the curves of distant galaxies. A skylight over her winter bedroom allows her to wake to the sweep of constellations, phases of the moon, and flavor of the dawn as seen through upper branches. On clear nights in summer, she sometimes moves her bed to a second-story outside deck where the giant trunks are almost within reach and the branches and needles sing with the breezes and dawn songs of birds.

"To tell the truth," she told me during a tour, "I don't know where my bedroom is. I migrate through here seasonally, and I like to disrupt routine. Waking up in a different spot shifts things for me." When her children or friends visit, or students stay over, she maintains an easy flexibility so that couples, families, and individuals get the rooms best suited to their wishes.

A second, newer building stands where a shed collapsed from snow load during a better-than-usual winter. It serves as a yoga studio, which she runs as Mad River Yoga. One end has a small apartment for guest overflow or visiting instructors. In addition, Mary has maintained her professional nursing career of thirty-five years and commutes to Burlington several days a week. The tiny chicken coop has been converted into an unlikely sauna. Beyond the sauna, the remains of three different tree forts recede into the hemlocks and yellow birches of the surrounding woods. As her children grew and became bolder in their explorations, the tree forts were built ever farther away to embrace the territories and adventures that required being out of sight of the home nest. Each reflects the childhood forays that, while measurable in mere hundreds of yards, may as well have been in distant terrain. The most recent remains at the farthest remove were the site of those first adventurous sleep-outs without supervision from "big people."

Long before dwindling resources and green-living consciousness made a virtuous statement of reusing materials and objects, Mary was a skilled scavenger. She has always liked old stuff and maintains an aversion to spending on new. She likes the stories of recycled things as much as the utilitarian aspects. At first I thought she meant stories that had meaning to her, but it turns out that just the assumption that stories are there is enough. A personal connection is not required, although it is certainly present in her most-cherished items. Her kids found an iron railing along a street in Montreal, tossed out to be picked up with other trash. They brought it to her for her summer sleeping deck—it keeps her from falling off. The ceiling over her downstairs tub and shower is a fine wooden door to nowhere. But if she ever needs a door she'll know where to get one and can easily replace the tub ceiling with boards from something and somewhere else. There is only one new window in her entire complex. People bring her stuff, just knowing that she is the one who will appreciate whatever it is. She presides over an efficient flow of goods that migrate to her. She doesn't need her own truck, or to invest time in a search, and only occasionally needs to hire someone with builder's skills to install various finds. The rest she does herself.

"Luckily, there is a guy named Cal who is very patient with my ideas and skilled at retrofitting. Sometimes I see his eyes roll beneath his hat brim when I request something way out there, but mostly he just nods and gets to solving and making things work," she says.

A fine wooden door affixed to a ceiling might have elicited an eye roll from Cal, but the means of flooding the yoga studio with natural light probably didn't. "I like light." Mary said while showing the second floor above the studio. There was a row of windows spanning the entire wall, and to share that abundance of light in the room below nearly a third of the floor was sheathed with clear polycarbonate greenhouse panels instead of floorboards. During daylight hours the studio below is full of glorious light. Not only does light pass through the clear panels, but the square tubes of airspace incorporated into them for structural and insulation value maximizes the heat retention of the room below. The other two-thirds of the floor is made of conventional pine boards and remains available for storage, foot traffic, or as an overflow sleeping loft for students and other guests.

An invitation to Mary's sauna gets interesting even before you arrive. The Mad River cuts its way through some impressive miniature gorges of metamorphosed, slate-like rock. It is all swirly and reoriented and dramatic. Towns tucked into the Mad River Valley tend to be at these little drops and constrictions that supported water-driven mills in earlier times. In the middle of Moretown, a steeply angled narrow bridge crosses the river and spans just such a gorge. Only two houses are on the far side, one of which is Mary's. Getting there has all the feel of entering an enchanted kingdom on the far side of a moat. Anyone with an imagination wouldn't be surprised if the ledges and pools below had gargoyles and dragons guarding them, and that what has the appearance of an ordinary bridge is likely a portal to a surprising place.

Various floods have returned the gorge to a near-natural state by washing out the former dam that made use of the narrow chasm. One remnant of a concrete wall shows a round arch where a penstock intake is now thirty feet above the present water level. Space beneath the bridge is likewise far more dramatic than when the most recent dam stilled the cascade to a calm holding pool just a few feet below the bridge decking. There is a fantastic swimming hole at the foot of the pitch, a clear greeny-deep pool that can be jumped into from the nearest ledge twenty-some vertical feet above. Mary's children learned to swim in that pool, and she herself is tickled to report that she hasn't yet reached that anticipated threshold when common sense and age suggest caution. She can still make the plunge from the ledge. Looking into the depths from above, I find I am proud of her, and I can imagine the surprise and admiration of the village kids and other swimmers whenever she takes the hair-flying-wild leap.

The chicken coop sauna perches on a slope not far from the kitchen door. While chickens may have found it

Stove pipe hints of another purpose for the former chicken coop.

commodious, for people it is rather small, yet surprisingly wondrous in its quirky way. Mary is trim and compact, but not miniature. As a yoga practitioner she has a limber grace, and she finds the diminutive dimensions adequate, so has remained minimalist in her retrofittings. She even avoided the most unpleasant task in its conversion to a sauna by hiring her son and one of his friends to scrub the place out. Upon hearing this I imagined the boys looking like bandits with bandanas tight over their mouths and noses to reduce the astringent eye-watering fumes of chicken poop, which are on a par, or even worse, than the considerable offenses cat pee can deliver. I envisioned them heroically attacking the fragrant history of chickens armed only with wire brushes and lots of soapy water. But it turned out that it wasn't that bad. The chickens had been gone long enough for all that to have evaporated, leaving only dust and debris that were easily shoveled and swept.

Mary found a couple of wide live-edge boards somewhere, and cut them to length for benches. A few sheets of thin composite insulation were around, so she took the corrugated roof off, put the panels down, and replaced the roof metal. There was enough insulation sheeting left over to tack it to the outside of most of the back. The rest is pretty much as Doyle made it, the boards now attractively weathered. Some remains of a fence cling to one side, the framing held together by the wire mesh, and the whole piece still held up by staples affixing it to the wall. It is not in the way, and has never revealed another use for re-purposing; so there it is, easier to ignore than remove. Besides, it projects forward enough to hang robes and towels on.

Essentially, this is a "found" sauna. A traditionalist would consider it a sauna in name only as it reveals none of the care in site selection, dimensions, flow of space and plan, and precision that is typically applied within the realm of Finnish ideals. But then, that is not Mary's point. One of the beauties of making do with what you have is an evolutionary flexibility regarding influence, and hybridizing, and making something one's own. Even the most stubborn stickler for tradition and properness would admit that the Mad River Chicken Coop Sauna is overflowing with the most important ingredient of all—love. It is loved so hard with unabashed zeal that many

Slim and tall former coal stove fits the tiny space perfectly.

of Mary's friends regard it as magical, a sorcerer's sauna, a place that radiates power.

Whatever time and money Doyle invested had long since been realized when it was still a chicken coop. The initial investment in the conversion to sauna was whatever the boys had been paid for the rigors of cleaning. Finding a stove was a bit more of a challenge and would introduce the biggest cash requirement. Given the dimensions, heating the space was not a problem, but finding a stove small enough was. The solution arrived in the form of a coal stove that was tall and slim. It could occupy a corner without taking up too much premium space. Better yet, it had a top that was removable, and a local fabricator was able to weld a cradle for the sauna stones. Used stove, $200; custom stone cradle, $160; boys' wages, not much (exact figures forgotten). All in all a fantastic deal. One would be hard pressed to create a useable sauna for a better bargain.

Of course, a firebox designed for lumps of coal has some limitations in the size wood it can accept, but once again, Mary's scavenger instincts prevailed. Rather than spend time cutting ridiculously short pieces of firewood, she simply drives to a local turning mill that manufactures round things out of hardwood. Once the products are finished and released from the lathes, a small piece of remnant wood that fits the chucks on the turning equipment is cut off each end. These ends are bagged up by the thousands, and since they are waste, are incredibly inexpensive. All Mary needs to do is show up at the mill, buy a couple of bags of ends, and lug them home. The ends are the size of goose eggs, perfectly seasoned (probably even kiln-dried), and fit the stove like a dream. As long as the supply stays steady at the mill, there is no need to be more than a few bushels of ends ahead, so storage requires nothing more than what fits beneath one end of the back bench.

When I arrive for sauna I find Mary and a friend, Claudia, in the kitchen. The conversation in progress is about energy work and sound as incorporated into a recent workshop Claudia was part of. She hands me a slice of pineapple and wraps up the flow of talk with Mary. In the pause, Mary rises to get some essential oils, a big bag of bath salts from the Dead Sea, and a mortar and grinding bowl to make the salt crystals a little finer. We take turns grinding the salt, sharing the preparation and infusing the act with whatever energy and subliminal components we are each contributing to this occasion. When Mary likes the size we've rendered, she offers us a rather diverse selection of essential oils to blend a scent from. This will be mixed with the salt, which in turn will be used as an exfoliating scrub and massage once we are hot and sweating freely in the sauna. Claudia chooses rosemary and sage, and I select sage and lavender. Our respective blends create a pleasing aroma and we each add the mix to a personal jar of the divided salt. A few drops of olive oil stretch the mix and extend the blend throughout the crystals.

As the sauna heats up, our conversation swings around to boundaries, comfort, friendship, and trust. While plenty of men have shared Mary's sauna and been introduced to various degrees of the ritualized bathing practices she has created, most of her sauna guests are women. Partly this is a reflection of a higher percentage of females participating in her workshops; the

Grinding Dead Sea bath salts to a finer grit.

Blending salt and essential oils in personal mix jars.

other part is that the evolution of her sauna style has grown more elaborate within the unfettered sisterhood of women's gatherings. I find I am basically occupying a position of "honorary woman" for the evening.

While Mary and I have benefited by building a bit of trust through correspondence, having met a few times and even shared a sauna at a mutual friend's house, Claudia and I have known each other for less than half an hour. Honorary gender-switcher or not, I'm a male participant and interviewer and photographer who has dropped out of the blue and wants to make the magic of Mary's sauna visible. So we have a bit of fun musing about how shocking and preposterous it would seem to the Puritan and Calvinistic sensibilities prevalent in an earlier New England trying to imagine that strangers were about to share a small hot place in their birthday suits. This turn of talk makes the particulars of establishing the rules regarding imagery and expected level of modesty within the photos to arise naturally and easily. When I confirm that each subject has total veto power regarding all images, Claudia's concerns vanish, making way for the refinements of Mary's rituals to embrace us. And the rules simplify my options. No photos in the sauna.

Regardless of where and how each of us has been raised, there is always some level of societal relativity regarding gender. The fact remains that to varying degrees, a male presence reduces the beautiful intimacy that exists in the women's sauna that is so gloriously experienced by women when they are by themselves.

This gift arises from a profound sense of safety and trust that blossoms, and that favors the unconscious companionable leaning upon one another, washing or braiding each other's hair, and scrubbing each other with complete generosity and grace. Conversations often flow and coil and leap like poetry, like improbable gymnastics, like dance. Edges are not much in evidence. This is a curved and spacious realm, full of expansion, and topics fly with their own centrifugal force.

Mary asked what a men's sauna is like. This caused me to realize that I'm so used to mixed sauna that I had to think back specifically to those times I had experienced a male-only occasion; and it is true there are differences. A lot more silent basking seems to take place, and topics tend to be more linear and narrow in detail. While we might whisk each other's backs with the *vihtas*, or rub the shoulders of someone in front on a lower bench, that is about the extent of communal nicety that I've personally experienced. Much of the time, our own council and space are maintained. At the time I didn't have a direct observational answer to her wondering if men alone experienced more freedom for expressing affection physically or conversationally.

With the sauna "seasoned" up to temperature, Mary provided us each with a bucket of cold rinsing water, drinking water, and, of course, our individual jars of fragrant salt. "You get the pink robe," she told me. "It's been worn

A guest and Mary head to the sauna, each with a bucket of cooling/rinse water, drinking water, and their personal jar of an exfoliating rub of bath salt and fragrant oils.

by a number of inspired visiting teachers, and a famous yogi or two. You'll be in good company." It was remarkably pink and bright. We couldn't help but laugh, it was so dazzling. It was so effervescent that I felt compelled to prance and leap between the living room and up the hill to the sauna.

The tiny space within the former chicken coop was surprisingly big enough for the three of us, despite requiring some care and choreography when shifting positions. We rotated between the hot spot, the medium spot, and the coolest bench, and in no time at all were hot enough to need to cool outside. During the next heating session we applied the glorious salt rub to our limbs and everywhere within easy reach. Backsides,

(In respecting Mary's request for no interior shots at her sauna, this image is from elsewhere and is in keeping with her practice but without the exfoliating salt and oil rub.)

upper arms, and shoulders were more effectively done by one another.

Salt crystals cleave with sharp angles. The abrasive scrub was positively delicious in the heat of fire and the flow of firm, strong hands giving and supremely relaxed muscles receiving. The blend of scented oils was like a symphony, and the slightest movement wafted the air around us in swirls and eddies of varying intensity. Even after cooling and rinsing, hints of aroma would rise from our skin like small bursts of magic.

Dusk was falling, the first stars emerging. Vermont in early April was in the thick of mud season. There was snow in the woods, although most of the fields and south-facing exposures were bare. In the next cooling, Claudia bade us leave the sauna steps to lie on the tingly frost materializing on last fall's snow-flattened grass. We were silent a while, admiring stars, lost in thoughts, waiting to perceive a chill. I heard a whisper from one of my companions: "It's been months since we could lie on the earth directly."

Were the season progressed into the heat of later spring, summer, or the still-warm leading edge of fall, Mary would have filled an outdoor claw-footed iron bathtub with water earlier in the day. If it were sunny, the water would have warmed up considerably, but still have favored the cooler end of the scale if scalding were the other end. This would have allowed a lovely full immersion rinse after the salt rub and sauna, all in the lush, full green of those seasons. Afterwards, a soothing and moisturizing shea butter rub would have concluded the luxurious sequence of the bath as Mary practices it.

During the cold and cooler seasons, the wood-heated warmth of the house would be retreated to after the final cooling session, and the shea butter would be applied without benefit of the outdoor rinse in the tub. But in either sequence of events, the resulting dimensionless euphoria may be as close to a heavenly swoon as one might get. I had hoped to revel a bit in recalling the moments of the evening when I retreated to my sleeping bag in the guest apartment of the yoga studio, but so complete and seamless was my surrender to a weightless slumber that those thoughts had to wait until morning. Then, just as dreams receded and daylight was coming on, the scent of lavender and sage reminded me where I was, and that the evening before had indeed been real.

Retreating across the slanted bridge from Mary's provided a reentry to a world where things were much more as they seemed. An early morning observer might have noticed someone departing by car to drive a short distance to catch the morning train to Burlington, and a few minutes later someone crossing the bridge on foot and entering a vehicle to drive who knows where. Invisible to the observer would be the gifts the "who-knows-where" driver was replaying in his mind: the palpable vision of a place where floors are made of light, doors in ceilings don't lead to accompanying hallways, and an incredible sauna looks remarkably like a chicken coop.

Our Lady of the Daffodils watching progress from one of the gardens.

CHAPTER 7

A Dream Becoming

Dream thresholds are sometimes hard to recall. At some point, transitions occur where dreaming something involves a decisive-enough step that the process becomes one of doing. Soon enough, those doings become the foundational makings of a project that seems already under way and gaining momentum.

For Fred Fauver, it might have been a spring day when we were walking his land ostensibly looking at the earliest flowers and chasing down the songs of arriving birds. His property is bounded by Chandler River, contains an esker topped by red pines, and skirts a wetland, so there was plenty to engage our curiosities. Fred is a thoughtful guy with myriad interests, and conversations jumped and twirled as they will on a fine day before the black flies emerge, and while the calls of wood frogs and spring peepers are dominant. It might have been that we actually spoke of sauna, and we might have thought this spot or that would be a good location. Or maybe not.

When I visited again it was clear that Fred had been thinking during the intervening time, and that the topic of sauna had indeed come up. "We need to finalize a site," he said. And we did. It had a view of the stream, required a long-enough stroll for the shedding of concerns, yet was close enough to the house no matter what the weather or what the temperature might be. "Let's have tea inside and I'll show you my sketches," he said.

The "sketches" were not simple doodlings from the nebulous front edge of an unfolding idea. These were drawn with an architect's scale, with notes in a neat hand indicating where ideas and features had been considered, reconsidered, and refined. This was now a project. There were goals to be met. And there were two witnesses outside the dreamscape who expected follow-through. One was a friend with a portable chainsaw mill scheduled to arrive the following week, the other was the code enforcement officer for the town of Pownal, Maine, soon to visit the site to recommend modifications or give his blessings. In addition, this was to be a fun project, recreational and even leisurely in pace. It would be done over time, no deadlines, fit-as-fit-can around the other parts of life. For starters, one of those parts involved knee-replacement surgery and the necessary recovery time. Fred would revert to dreaming while waiting to rebound enough to scamper around a worksite with stamina and grace.

Fred Fauver—craftsman who built his own home and woodworking shop and later began to dream of a sauna.

"This might be the spot. I'm pretty sure I favor this place."

Answers to questions that arise as ideas unfold inform balance and direction of design.

An abundance of red pine near the site and a friend with a portable chainsaw mill…

...provided for materials that were stacked and drying near the woodworking shop.

A pre-build near the shop allowed for extension cords to reach power tools and for precision fitting of the piece-on-piece framing for the primary structure.

Eleven-year-old Iris was happy to lend a hand marking just where her grandfather should make the cuts.

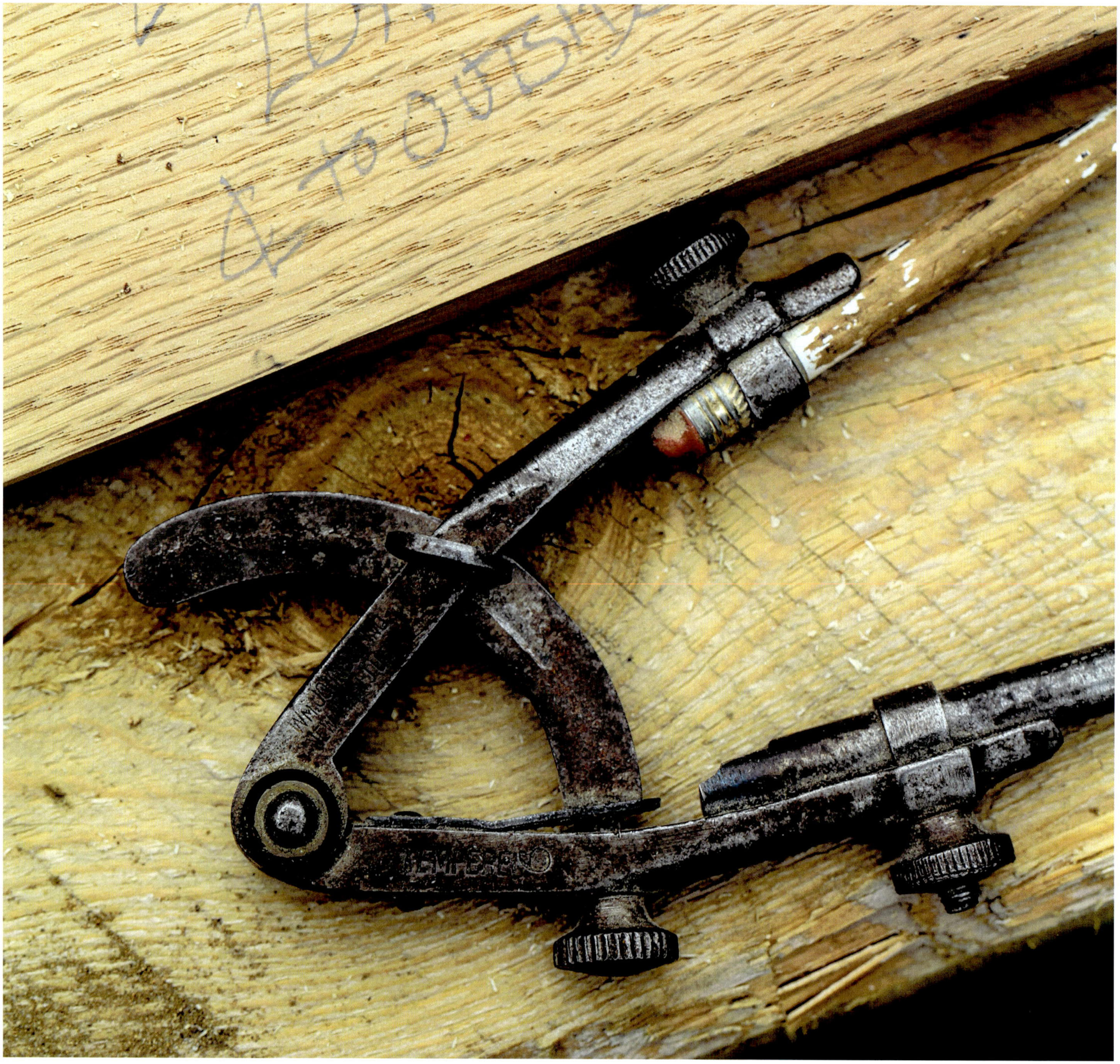

With everything numbered and dissembled it was time to move materials to the site...

...and establish true plumb and level for the building to begin.

91

As progress revealed the actual shape of things to come, further questions would arise that might involve changes to the drawn plans, such as where window placement would best serve people on the benches.

Where would the wall between the hot room and changing room best divide the space?

Smaller components were more efficiently built in the heated and well-organized shop and moved to the site when ready for installation.

The completion of each new stage palpably increased excitement and inspiration for next steps.

Modifying a window between the hot room and dressing room after a friend made a stained-glass window that turned out a little bigger than the framing.

97

With the installation of a stove that Fred already had, modified with a cradle welded by a local fabricator to hold the stones, the first firing was tantalizingly close.

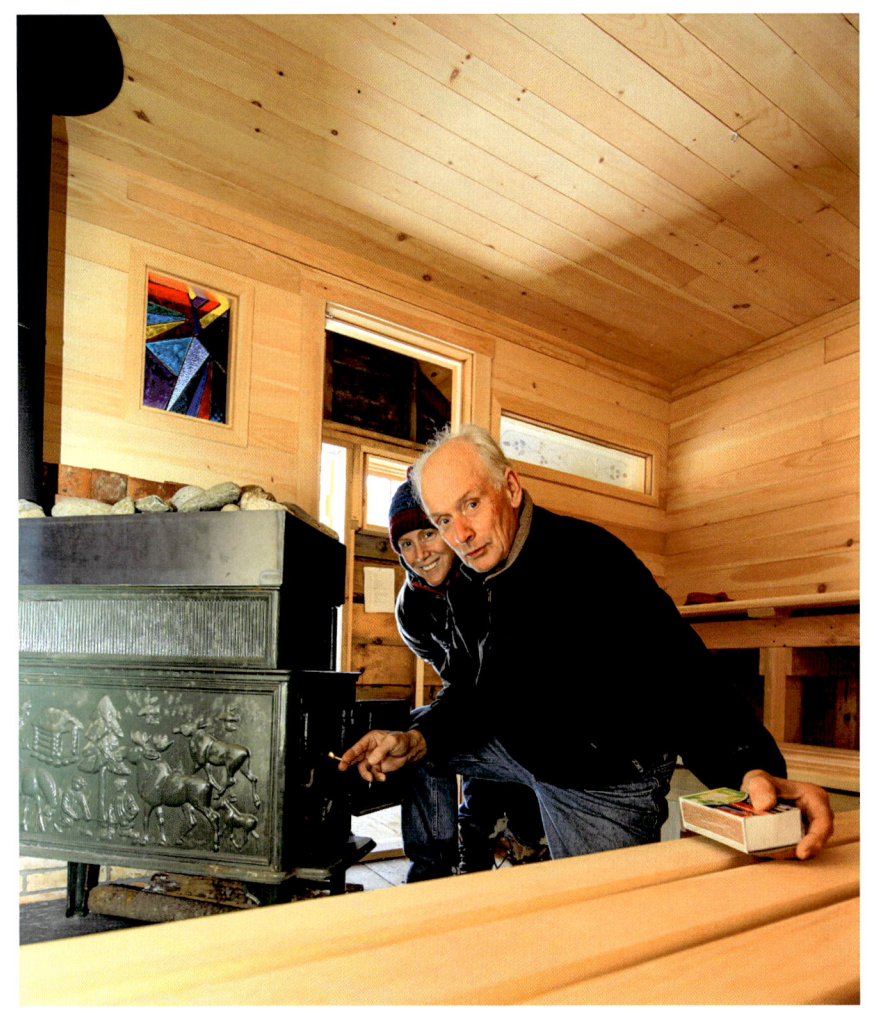

Daughter Allyson, visiting from Montana, made the first firing extra special as she had been following news of progress from 2,000 miles away…

...and wouldn't have missed sharing the moment of first smoke for anything.

What a glorious celebratory firing! There were few enough present, so all had a place on the top benches for the best heat.

Allyson blissful in the radiance of her Dad's dream.

With each announcement of a firing, "birds of a feather flock together" at Fred's. As the community of regular and occasional revelers grows, there is still only one among us who can claim a quite literal affinity to the saying.

As the number of firings grew, a spontaneous consensus emerged, and folks began referring to the sauna as "The Box," although the jury is still out and Fred is hopeful that an even better name will emerge.

105

106

Ever patient, the garden sculpture observed progress through the seasons, starting as Our Lady of the Daffodils, transitioning to Our Lady of the Snows, and finally emerging again knee deep in daffodils.

"See you next Saturday," has replaced "next firing" among the regulars. Even if Fred is not around, he is happy to have a guest host take care of keeping the weekend firings uninterrupted.

With firings in full swing and June tipping toward solstice, there are occasional sightings of Ladies of the Summer delighting in the lush green of the season.

Elise dancing to Stephen's flute while waiting for a proper entry temperature.

The Chandler River cooling pool below the sauna proved to be over eight feet deep even in low water.

Some time later Fred wrote that he had been re-reading The Tea Book by Okakura Kazuko and remarked how easily one could substitute the word sauna for tea room. Then in the spirit of his reading he let me know a firing was almost ready. "The sauna heats. The path is thick with autumn leaves."

113

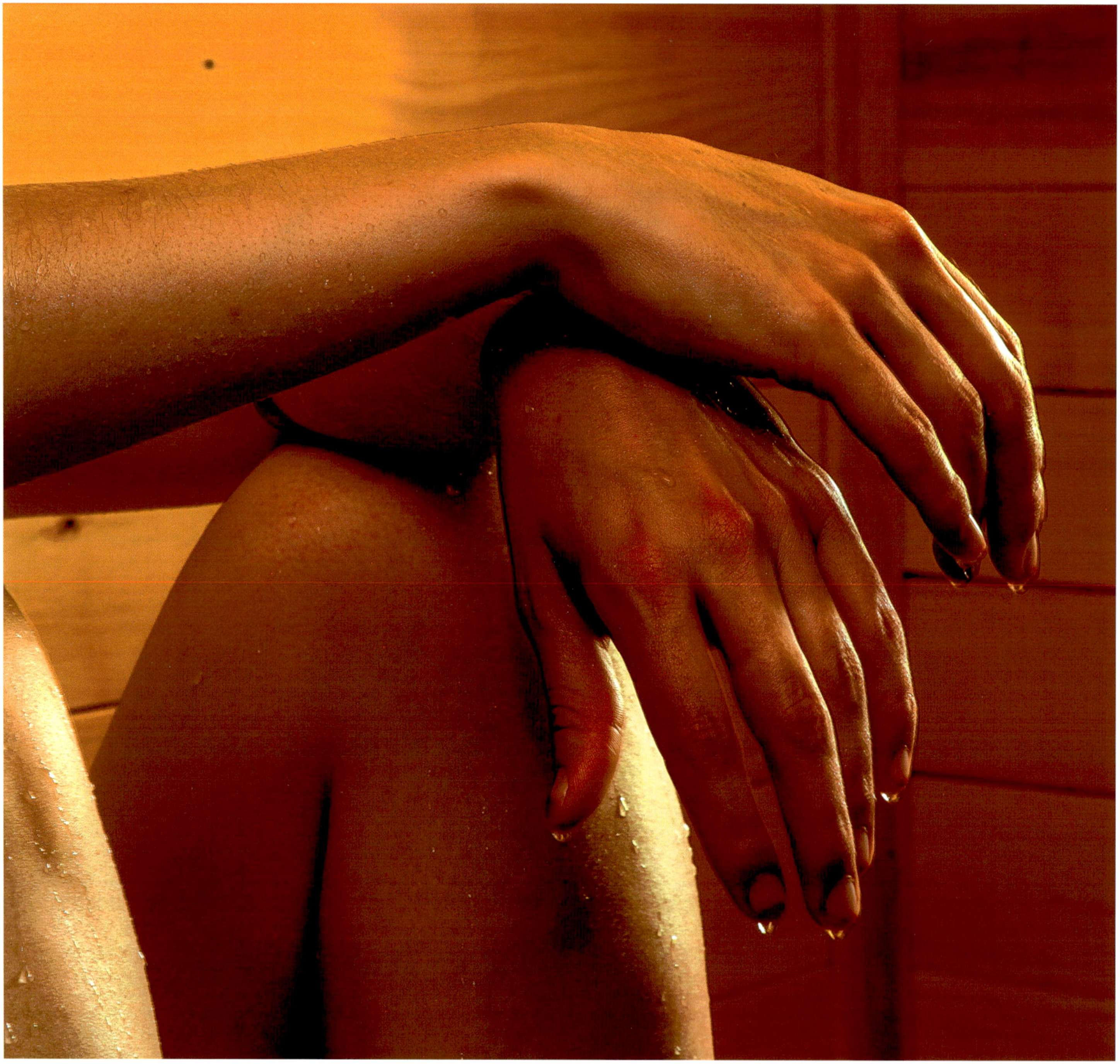

CHAPTER 8

Home Sauna on the Wilson Stream

Step 1) Settle in a lovely place.

I was one half of "that strange couple that moved to town." There are only 139 people in Willimantic, Maine, so news travels at about the same speed a clap of thunder can roll down the Wilson Stream valley during a storm full of lightning. Friends were quick to report the funniest ripples of gossip, but I actually heard part of a discussion first hand while gassing up at a convenience store in Monson, the next town over. When I entered to pay, I caught the tail end of two guys talking who didn't know it was me they were talking about: "Yeah, they put that nice new building up at the road, but they still live down by the river in a tent." Long pause. "I'll be damned. Kinda old for that, aren't they?"

It often takes a while to sneak as close to perfection as you can get, but the time and effort are invariably worth it. In the case of choosing where to live, all considerations take on heightened importance commensurate with the seriousness of any such long-term plan. So we made a wish list. We wanted to be within a half-hour drive of Dover-Foxcroft, which is just big enough so that banking, groceries, hardware, a hospital, and even a health food store are available. As wilderness trip guides running canoe trips in spring, summer, and fall and snowshoe and toboggan trips in the winter, we needed a base central to the primary jumping off points for the Maine North Woods. Dover-Foxcroft provided a perfect hub. It is within reasonable range of the Bangor airport for trip guests who fly in, is situated centrally at the southern edge of the North Woods, and is the shire town of a county that is nearly as big as the state

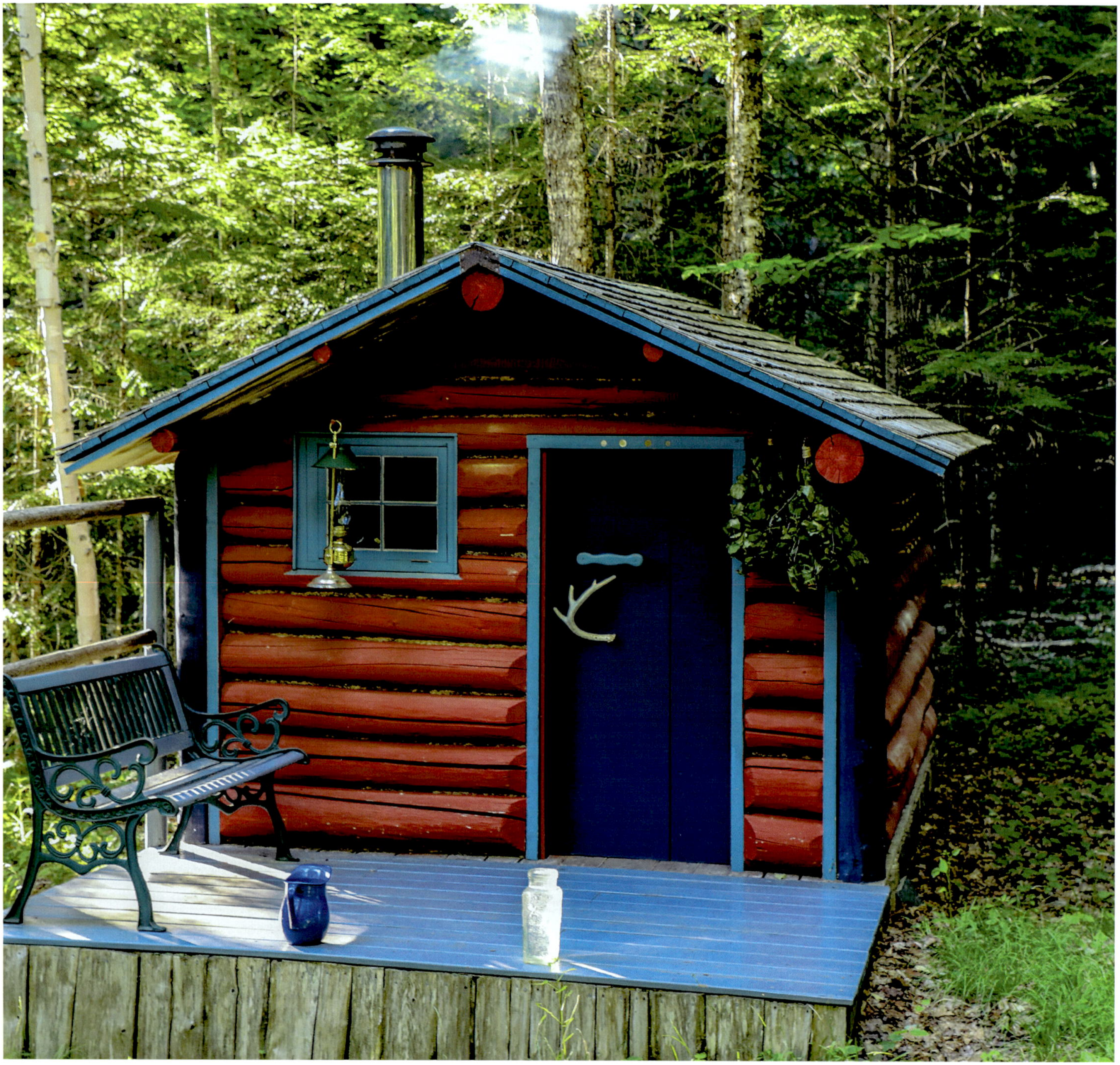

117

of Connecticut but with fewer than 18,000 people scattered throughout. In addition to the aspects favoring Maine, the location is likewise central to the routes to Quebec and Labrador for longer Canadian canoe and snowshoe trips that require true large-scale wilderness farther north. Should the desire for something available only within a cityscape beguile, Quebec City is closer than Boston.

The search for just where to settle started with a set of dividers, the kind with a pin on one leg and a pencil clamped to the other. They were spread to a span equaling twenty miles according to the scale in the corner of a road map. The pin was placed in Dover-Foxcroft and the pencil traced an arc on the north side of Routes 6 and 15. Despite being only halfway up the state, these combined roads provide the most northerly paved route that traverses the full width of a region with few east-west passages. The resulting pencil line encompassed some promising country, including the tiny town of Willimantic.

With an ideal region determined it was time to apply what we called the fussy factors. We needed a road with power lines along it, some woods, a spring for drinking water, and, just to avoid compromising on anything, some shoreline preferably on a stream rather than a pond or lake. If a stream could be found it would be nice if it had enough current and drop so that there would be some mild rapids or at least riffles that would make a little sound. The sound would provide pleasing news about water levels throughout the seasons, be soothing as background music, and, most importantly, would eclipse the noise of traffic on any roads within earshot, or the power mowers and weed whackers of adjacent neighbors. If we could find a place with 50 percent of what we hoped for, and an owner willing to sell, it would be in the running for consideration.

Sometimes when courting luck the results are not just good, but unbelievably grand. It took some patience that stretched for several years, but when things fell into place, our fortune was so precise as to be alarming, at least to New Englanders who are habitually suspicious of overabundance and perfection without any apparent strings attached.

Just beyond one of the bridges in Willimantic a road headed up a hill, turned to dirt after a few hundred yards, and had the requisite poles carrying phone and power lines a little ways north out of town. An older woman just up the hill had eleven acres she was willing to sell, and the parcel went from road edge to the river. At river edge there was a spring. Above the spring was a site we thought would be perfect to set up a permanent wall tent. Beavers had already established a trail up the bank where we would get wash water from the river, drinking water from a spring, and have access to a pool just deep enough for a full emersion "swim." Over time, our neighbor decided she liked us well enough to sell six more acres of land, and later yet, another four or five acres.

There is an island in the river nearly the full width of our frontage that has enough fir, spruce, and hemlock on it so that you can't see across to the far side even in winter when the hardwood leaves are down. Should land on that side ever be sold, and if someone were to build there, we would remain out of sight of each other. River bed cobble and boulders create the perfect amount of water music: not too soft during drought conditions and not too loud at moderate or even high-water levels.

An office, facility for equipment, and a shop was built at road edge, while at river edge we set about framing up a floor, low log walls, and a peeled pole frame for a twelve-by-twenty foot wall tent. At first we used our ears for windows, since you could hear through the canvas, and went outside to look if something interesting was unfolding. But soon enough we cut out a section of wall and made a small dining alcove, complete with a

119

four-by-seven foot Plexiglas window looking over the river. We also sewed in some smaller, clear rolled plastic windows for more light in the bedroom.

Soon enough, our previously puzzled neighbors were able to correct whatever their imaginings pictured when they heard about the tent down by the river. Enough people actually walked down to visit and could then accurately report on the more substantial presence of the permanent tent big enough for a queen sized bed, Vermont Castings wood stove, three-burner gas range, gas lights, kitchen table, furniture, and an iron kitchen sink. After twenty-some years, everyone appears to have gotten used to the idea that the building is for work, public interaction, and computer and phone access, and that the tent is home. There is just enough distance between the two to limit visitors to exactly who we are excited to see. Serendipitously, the depth of the river valley is such that the invasive reach of the nearest cell phone tower is rendered mute, yet the signal from National Public Radio is there for those programs that are eagerly and happily listened to.

The trail between river edge and road is just long enough for one to plan their day "up above" while commuting to the shop or office. By the same token, it provides a long-enough stroll at the other end of the day for work concerns to be left behind and not imported to the sanctuary of home. The sauna came later, and provides a splendid crowning touch.

Step 2) Build a Sauna.

Only one thing equals the magic and extended circle of warmth provided by friends who share their saunas: a return to the homegrown joys of one's own. No matter how humble or grand, the home sauna is loved the best. Because it is always ready to be fired whenever an occasion arises, it can't help but accumulate the stories that enhance depth and meaning. As with any beloved, time and proximity and long familiarity grows an ever-deepening bond. The Wilson Stream Sauna became animate at some point during the building process; at least, that is when I started talking to it out loud. I recall being startled because I heard my own voice ask it a question when a building decision was in the balance. All these years later, I still greet it as I walk up to it, and thank it when departing. Occasionally, a visiting guest warms my heart immeasurably when they spontaneously and unconsciously address it out loud. It all started with a single stone.

The stone arrived in the mail. For three consecutive winters, friends in Ely, Minnesota, had hosted Alexandra and me during January while we were leading a couple of snowshoe and toboggan trips in the Boundary Waters Canoe Area Wilderness. Not only did they provide a field office and trip launching base, but they maintained a gorgeous sauna in their basement. Between trips there was always time for conversations and philosophizing while enjoying the sauna together. It wasn't far into that first season that Scott and Wende were the first to hear us say with unbridled conviction, "We're going to build one of these."

We hadn't been back in Maine a week when a small box arrived in our mailbox. Within was a stone. One of those self-adhesive Post-it notes was affixed with a simple message: "Get Going." When we peeled the note off, we discovered a beautiful otter in relief upon the stone.

I'd like to report that we hustled right to it. But, of course, dreams often take some time, and need to be fit in and shaped around other details. We kept the stone on the dining table so it would always be visible and more powerful at reminding and inspiring. The next season of winter trips in Boundary Waters rolled around again, and by then we knew that one of the sauna stove companies was in Bruce Crossing, a small town on Michigan's Upper Peninsula. Our route to Ely would take us right through there, and, true to its name, there was a cross road that intersected M28, the main east/west road across the northern part of the UP. Less than a mile north of the junction was the stove shop. We entered to look at several varieties of wood-fired models that would suit our plans.

While not expensive as stoves go, the options were still a lot of money for us, and we had spent a fair amount of time discussing economizing by just retrofitting a simple bull-dog style stove we already had with some sort of structure that would cradle stones and thus become a sauna stove. We told the proprietor we'd give it some thought, and perhaps stop in again on our way back through at the end of the month. While it didn't take long to walk from the welding shop and display area back to the van, it was long enough for all the reasons that a stove built to a specific purpose is probably a bargain to sink into our heads. Before we had driven half the length of the parking lot, we grinned at each other and agreed to pick up a stove on the way back to Maine.

Finally, we had "gotten going" as Scott and Wende had admonished us nearly a year earlier. We had the first stone, a stove, and a future site picked out. Stones are light and portable in the sizes appropriate for a sauna stove. The stove was neither light nor portable. More than fifteen hundred feet of trail through the woods had to be traversed to get the stove to the site, but a solution materialized in the form of twelve visiting Winter Ecology students and their professor from College of the Atlantic.

The sauna site was near the tent by the river, free of the road and immersed within quiet, appealing surroundings. When the students arrived, we proposed the stove-moving plan as a way for them to get the two-hour drive to Willimantic out of their systems before settling in for their weekend of fieldwork. They were happy to help. In no time at all we had the stove levitated onto a sled, and with a few people pulling, a few pushing, and

Interior dimensions at eight by ten feet are perfect for both a solo sauna…

the rest stabilizing everything from the sides, we slithered the load through the woods like some multi-legged nivian caterpillar. When the route got steep and twisty, there were enough extras to serve as brakes and additional stabilizers. We settled the stove on log skids and

wrapped it in a tarp for however long the wait might be until it had a building to occupy.

Midway through the following June, when the bark slips easily, we began to cut and peel logs. Although the ideal

…and the more crowded benches of a social sauna filled with winter ecology students.

species, cedar and spruce, are common in the region, we did not have either in quantity or quality on our land. What we did have in abundance, including many of a perfect size, were bigtooth aspen, one of three species of poplar in the area. The site for the sauna was perched at the crest of a secondary terrace up from the river edge. That slope had a stand of poplar that had grown fast and tall reaching for the light. Some trunks were so straight, with so little taper, that three logs would come from a single tree. Diameter preference randomized which trees were felled, and the end result was a perfect selective thinning not concentrated in any one area. Most of the stand was composed of trees too big for our needs, and those that were too small, or crooked, maintained a desirable uneven mix of sizes and ages left standing.

Decisions regarding dimensions had to be finalized now that trees were being felled. We peeled the bark as high as diameter minimums suggested and left the leafy tops on to speed up the drawing of moisture from the sap wood. Once the leaves withered from lack of nutrition, we'd cut the logs to length and rack them for further drying at the building site.

Dimension considerations are simple if you know the number of participants you are building for. The farther out along a sliding scale you go, the more speculative and uncertain things become. One thought was that the building should be small enough so that a person could take a solo sauna without feeling they were being extravagant with burning firewood. Probably there would be two to six participants most of the time, assuming there might be a few "regulars" we'd notify anytime it was fired up. We also knew that at least a few times a year there would be events that should accommodate more. We hosted two contra dances annually that came to be known as "Canoe Hall Dances." People who travelled a distance to attend the potluck and dance were invited to camp along the river and partake of a big pancake feed in the morning. In addition to the dances, we expected other events would materialize and provide increased numbers who might enjoy a sauna.

In the end, our decision was to make the interior dimensions eight by ten feet. To save on log length and speed up the building process, we elected not to have notched and fitted corners, which, while intricate and fun to create, take a lot more time and require a foot or more of additional length at each end for the overlap. Despite the guesswork on potential numbers, we lucked out and achieved perfect balance. A solo sauna is splendid, twelve fit comfortably, and fifteen fit tightly seated. Just for the record, at one of the dances, seventeen fit due to a couple of people willing to stand near the stove while spinning in place to avoid scorching themselves in any one spot. With the record established and witnessed, a laughing mass evacuation took place and good sense has prevailed ever since. It is a simple matter for folks to alternate cooling and heating sessions when there is too large a crowd to fit all at once.

The bench structure is such that two can stretch out on the upper benches in total luxury, complete with head rests. Four can enjoy full-stretched relaxation, if all bench levels are used. And six, eight, and even ten can sit nicely. Beyond that, some care must be taken to avoid jabbing a neighbor with a knee or elbow. As we suspected, there are a number of occasions when a crowded social sauna happens. The Winter Ecology class usually has sauna participants during the annual field trips. And

Inspirational otter stone and raven design on the center slate tile of the spark guard.

various college outing clubs make a spring freshet run of the Big Wilson in kayaks and whitewater canoes in late April, when the water is still wintery cold, there is remnant snow in the woods, and the season is likely to be delivering a cold spring rain. If someone is around to fire up when any whitewater paddling groups pass by, it is quite a marvelous treat for them to be able to jump into a sauna a short while after peeling out of a cold wet suit at the end of their run. The bridge in town is just a half mile downstream, and by the time everyone has changed, loaded gear, and driven up the hill to the Canoe Hall, the sauna is ready. Sometimes you can hear a bit of a stampede charging down the trail just before the chilled paddlers arrive, desperate to pile inside and absorb some heat.

Other luck factors fell into place during the building time. A friend across town who has a small sawmill was eager to saw all of the framing and planking materials. He milled the joists and floor and ceiling boards from cedar for the fragrance and rot resistance. Another friend who is a wood-and-canvas canoe builder supplied us with perfectly clear cedar for the benches and headrests. And there were plenty of various sized rocks in a small brook just a few yards behind the site for creating a solid foundation.

Another friend, John Tatko, continues in the family business of Sheldon Slate, which has quarries and mills in Vermont and New York and owns the final remaining slate enterprise in Monson, the next town over from Willimantic. When I asked if I could get some slate for the spark guard to go in front of the stove he got intrigued. "Hey, you draw," he said. "Make a simple design and I'll show you how to sandblast it onto the centerpiece. You can have it either depressed or in relief."

To honor the Finns of Monson and the local quarrying history, the center tile is of the famous dark Monson Slate. For color, the bracketing slates are burgundy and gray-green and come from the Vermont quarries. I drew a simple, stylized raven looking back over its shoulder with a sweeping wing beneath the head and bill. Not only is the raven a wonderful circumpolar bird, but the choice refers to my late friend Bill Osgood, who first introduced me to Finnish sauna in the hills of Northfield, Vermont, at Kelirikko Sauna (Broken or Rough Ground Sauna), which he had helped build with neighbors. Bill liked to bestow names, and thus called his homestead and surrounding woodlot Ravencroft. Eventually, when he made his own sauna, it was situated just across his driveway, near a farm pond and incorporated into a pole barn. Hrafn Sauna he called it, *hrafn* being the Icelandic word for raven.

In the end, it all came together gloriously. The sauna perches in a lovely setting like a jewelry box. I was so excited to have had a part in making the little building that I would stroll up there occasionally with a cup of tea and sit at the base of a nearby tree and admire it, as if I needed to make sure it was really there, and as beautiful as I thought.

Other niceties have emerged over time. A gravity-feed pipeline from upstream in the brook behind delivers running water in all but the driest of summers, and after freeze-up in the fall and winter. The rocks in the cradle on the stove all have significance. One from the home river is not just a pleasing stream rock, but one of the scouring stones the current whirls around within one of the natural kettle holes in the slate ledges and falls that punctuate the river just upstream. Rivers

As the open leads in the river ice expand in March and early April, a cold plunge is safe and invigorating during the transition season.

of the various canoe routes are represented: the St. John, Allagash, and West Branch of the Penobscot in Maine; the Grand and Attikonak of Labrador. Once, toward the end of a two-month snowshoe and toboggan crossing of the Ungava Peninsula in Quebec, I added a rock from the George River to a nearly empty food pack. Friends have brought others as gifts: one from the Agawa pictograph site on the north shore of Lake Superior, others from the coast of Downeast Maine. In the place of honor, the most visible spot, is the first one, the otter stone.

A propensity for simplicity has been rewarded with several unforeseen delights. While some saunas are quite elaborate with perhaps a cooling area, washroom, shower, and dressing room attached; the Wilson Stream Sauna is simply the sauna itself and an uncovered deck in front. In this way the seasons, time of day, and the immediate world are included as an important part of each firing. The short stroll from the tent to the sauna is as pleasing and significant as the rest of the experience, as is the "air bath" walk to the stream in summer when cooling is in the water. Whenever I scan through the entries in the Sauna Log, there is always reference to whatever is timely: the singing of thrushes, phase of the moon, green shade of summer, blue evening light of

Photo by Alix W. Hopkins.

With the Wilson Stream so close, cooling plunges between hot room rounds are never far away. (Bottom photos by Alix W. Hopkins)

winter, even a barred owl that was calling and landed in a red maple so close above the deck we were able to watch each other. Gray tree frog songs, rain, lightning, thunder, snow, wind, and stars seem to be regularly acknowledged. An entry recalls softly falling snow as we cooled on the deck in the hush of a winter night as "my shoulders and breasts being kissed by angels."

Because the door is proportionately small, as befits such a tiny structure, everyone but kids and our petite Penobscot friend Jennifer, who fits under with an inch to spare, must duck to enter or exit. This means everyone bows to the room and anyone already in it upon entry, and bows to the greater world when exiting renewed and purified. To honor some of the wildlife of the north, a series of holes sized to accept certain Canadian coins are set above the door. The two dollar coin depicts a polar bear, the one dollar a loon, a quarter has a caribou, and the five-cent piece a beaver. One guest, while admiring the coins, exclaimed: "Oh, what a nice address. This sauna is at three dollars and thirty cents Wilson Stream Way."

The dance gatherings inevitably attract a high percentage of musical people, and once a dancer who was a trip leader from one of the famous Midwestern canoe camps taught us all a round that not only had the usual circular harmonics, but a structure that mimicked two voyageur canoes passing each other while traveling in opposite directions. She coached us in the French lyrics and how to quietly build the distant approach, rise to the full crescendo as the two canoes pass each other in mid-chanson, then fade as the distance grows between. As it happened, the people responsible for the final fading verse were on the bench section just opposite the stove. There is a curved sheet-metal heat shield in the corner behind the stove, and in the small confines of the sauna, the shield acted as a reverberator that projected an ethereal choir over us as the final voices softened to silence. In that moment, despite the intense heat, there was a brief incredible chill that embraced us. We stayed quiet a spell while that magic settled, and only in the morning learned that everyone present felt that ghostly pulse like a cool, fresh breath conjured from the northern reaches of canoe country.

Soon after the sauna had its fifteenth birthday, I contemplated staining the exterior with solid colors to spiff things up. The exposed deck and railing had always been stained a pale blue reminiscent of the blue in the Finnish flag, but I had left the logs and all other wood surfaces unfinished to honor the trees that provided the materials. For a long time, the peeled logs held a fresh brightness, and the unplaned lumber looked suitably in keeping with the forest. But by the time I replaced the cedar shingles on the roof, everything was weathering to a mosaic of darkening blotchy patches of inconsistent color, and it seemed a good time for upkeep.

That is when I was seduced by the color chart for solid color stain at a local hardware store. There was an off-red called Indian Corn that fell somewhere between burgundy and barn red. There was a deep blue with a hint of purple called Newburyport Blue. Indian Corn had enough red to complement the greens of summer, and would be as bright and festive as high bush cranberries amidst the white of winter snow. The vertical corner logs and the door took the deep blue stain as if to recall the closed gentians growing in the bogs of Labrador and hint of the blue shade of winter days and the purple twilight of snowy evenings. Together, the colors snap into view like a crisp pattern on a dancer's skirt. Serendipitously, it reminds European visitors of a touch of old world esthetics.

Somewhere along the way, we started dedicating some of the splashes of water to the stones as a ceremonial part of any Wilson Stream Sauna firing. This is often done aloud, and many guests quickly fall into the pattern, adding their own blessings. It is a nice way to encourage thoughtfulness and generosity and create a formal pause to ease the occasion to a slower, more reverent pace. Many more dedications are undoubtedly cast silently. Always there is one of thanks to the Finnish traditions and people who have perfected and refined such an incredible gift to the world, and another for the *Tonttu*, the spirit that comes to occupy a well-loved, happy sauna. If one has not already taken up residence, the welcoming gesture is always there to greet it when it does.

Yukiko "Yuki" Oyama divides her time between Japan and Brooklyn, New York. She is an enthusiastic member of the Sauna Association of Japan, and her various sauna quests have taken her across the United States and to Finland. Early in her sauna sojourning, I was happy to host her on a visit to several Maine saunas, where she was delighted to take full charge of the preparations, firing, and enjoyment of her first log sauna experience along the Wilson Stream.

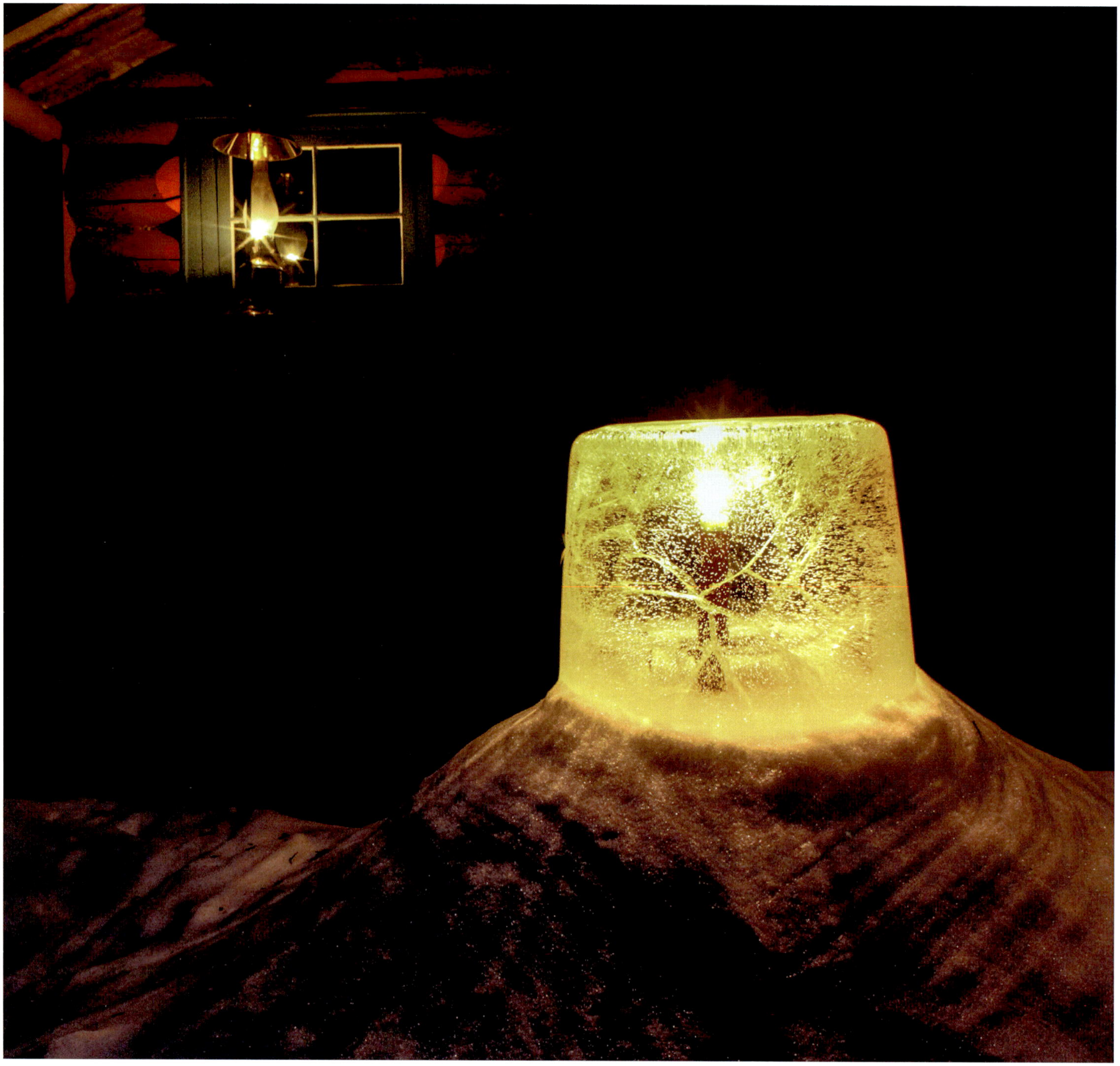

CHAPTER 9

Making Ice Lanterns

Anyone with a sauna in an area where subfreezing temperatures are the norm in winter will likely become an enthusiastic maker of ice lanterns. These are simple and fun to make, remarkably attractive, and add immeasurably to the esthetics and ceremonial joy of winter saunas.

The tradition in Canada and America came with any number of northern European immigrants, but seems to be most often attributed to Scandinavians and Russians. I first heard of them in Vermont as "Norwegian candle lanterns" and in Ely, Minnesota, as "Finnish ice lanterns"; it seems I also read something about "Russian ice lights" in an ethnographic account or perhaps a novel.

The ingredients are simple and readily available. All you need is time, sub-freezing temperatures, a source of water, some buckets, an ice pick or pointed knife, and candles. It is also handy to have a larger basin that can be filled with hot water to speed up the process of removing the lanterns from the buckets that formed them during the freezing process.

While the process is simple, there are some points that make things easier. Flared stainless steel or plastic buckets with smooth interiors and no seams are best. Fill the buckets with water and leave them outside when a good cold snap provides an opportunity. The water will begin to freeze from the surface exposed to air, and the edges of the bucket. In deep cold, well below zero, four hours may be all you need to achieve a good thickness. If it is warmer, the time required increases, and eight to twelve or more hours may be necessary to achieve desired thickness. The longer exposure time lends itself to an all-day or overnight process, so you can be doing other things, without risking the water freezing solid and the ice deforming or breaking the buckets as it expands.

The ice will form quickest at the surface exposed to air, slightly slower where the water is in contact with the sides of the bucket, and slowest at the bottom of the bucket. Your curiosity will keep you checking progress far too frequently during your first attempt, but as you become more experienced you will develop a more accurate sense of timing for when to check. A minimum

Chipping the hole to pour remaining water out when desired thickness is achieved.

sidewall thickness of half an inch is necessary, while an inch or inch and a half will reduce breakage during handling and last longest when exposed to the dry cold air of winter where sublimation will slowly erode the sides. Thicker, more robust lanterns may actually survive a short thaw or winter rain that might cause thinner ones to vanish.

The faster the freezing process, the clearer the ice will be, while the slower the process, the more gas bubbles, swirls, and cloudiness will be incorporated yielding a translucent lantern. You can usually gauge thickness by peering down through the surface ice where it contacts the bucket edge. When the desired thickness is reached, it is time to get a pointed knife or ice pick and carefully chisel down through the surface in two spots near the edges on opposite sides of the bucket. Once these two holes are made, you can pour the remaining water out, leaving only the shell of ice frozen to the bucket. Another trick is to make these holes large enough to hook your thumb in one and your index finger in the other for a firm grip to help ease the ice lantern from the bucket. For lanterns that are thicker, a single large hole can be chipped for pouring out the water without fear of cracks or breakage.

135

A large basin filled with warm water greatly speeds up the separating of the ice from the bucket. By swirling and rotating each ice-lined bucket through this warm bath, just enough melt will occur at the bucket and ice interface to release the ice. If you insert your fingers through the drain holes as mentioned above, you have both leverage and a solid grip to gently extract the ice with a simultaneous twist-and-pull motion. You can also simply leave the buckets standing in a warm environment for a short while.

Now you have clear or translucent globes for your candle lanterns. What was the top surface during formation will become the bottom of the lantern. Not only did the flared bucket shape facilitate extraction from the bucket, but once inverted, the base is now wider than the top for increased stability.

What is now the top of the lantern was formed at the bottom of the bucket where the ice is thinnest. This is handy, because you need to carefully chip an opening large enough to insert your hand for candle placement and lighting. A sponge with warm water run around the newly chipped rim will smooth it up nicely. The lantern is then ready to be positioned in the snow, and then you can place a candle inside.

Expect some attrition, and make more lanterns than you anticipate wanting. The lanterns are breakable during extraction from the buckets, while drain holes or top and bottom openings are being chipped, and by collision or being dropped. While you can often weld a simple clean break back together with water, sometimes a full shattering loss occurs and you need to create a replacement by starting over.

There is one other refinement to consider. If you use tall candles, you will need to replace them less frequently. By chipping the bottom out of the lantern, you can push the candle down into the underlying snow until the tip is a third or halfway down from the rim of the lantern. This is pleasing visually, as well as protective of the flame from any wind or breezes. Next time the candle is to be lit, simply pull it out, push a little snow into the hole, and reset the candle to the desired height. Thus, a

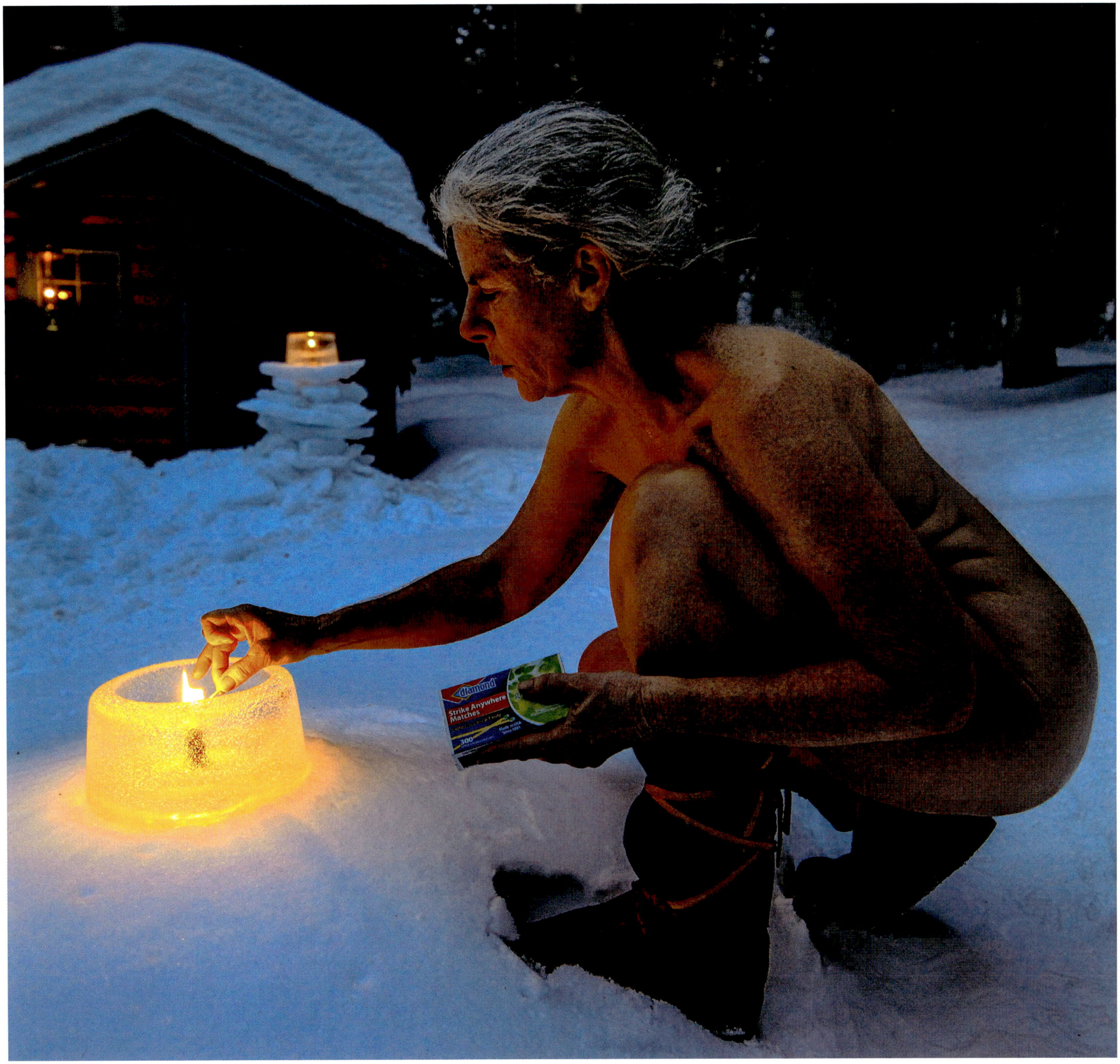
diamond
Strike Anywhere
Matches
300

twelve-inch candle is completely adjustable, and may last three or four lightings. A votive candle, or any similarly short one, will be good for only one event if left burning an hour or two.

Finnish friends have told me that red lanterns can be made by using water that beets were cooked in. Another friend in Vermont makes spherical and other-shaped lanterns by filling balloons with water and then peeling the thin rubber away once the proper level of freezing has occurred. This allows for the creation of complex and recurved shapes that could not be extracted from rigid containers.

A line of ice lanterns along the trail or near the entry of a sauna adds an immeasurably magical aura to a snow-clad scene. With the snow reflecting the light upward, and the ice refracting the glow of candles directly, the sight of your companions swaying toward the sauna in the soft lantern light has all the dreamy resonance of a gorgeous, transcendent dance.

CHAPTER 10

"See You on the Bench":
A revival of public sauna in Minneapolis

The blossoming of the 612 Sauna Society in Minneapolis, Minnesota, is at once miraculous and mundane. The miracle has to do with timing and vision. The mundane has to do with organic processes that were probably inevitable, much the way a volunteer seed in a compost bin might yield an exceptional strain of vegetable that ends up being desirable and thus shared garden-to-garden in ever-widening circles. From subtle origins, magic has a way of making itself known, even if the complications of germination take place mysteriously. In the surprise accompanying an unfolding blossom, it is easy to forget that many ingredients have led to that moment.

John Pederson is a key ingredient. A couple of seemingly small events put a kink in his trajectory when he was a college student. He grew up in St. Cloud, Minnesota, attended a Catholic school, and entered the School of Journalism at the University of Wisconsin in Madison. Early on he spotted an under-publicized application for the Brittingham Viking Scholarship, a five-month exchange program in Scandinavia, funded by a university alumnus. Intuitive leaps were made.

Somehow, John knew he had to apply, and with the unfounded zeal that can open so many doors, he simply *knew* his attempt would succeed. He had another intuitive leap on the way to the interview requested on the strength of his written application. He dressed up as best he could, suddenly nervous about speaking to a bunch of august alumni who would decide his fate. He passed a shoe store, causing him to consider a wardrobe weakness. He soon found himself inside trying on a pair of fancy shoes a college kid could never afford. But the shoes cast a spell upon him that promised confidence he thought might be helpful.

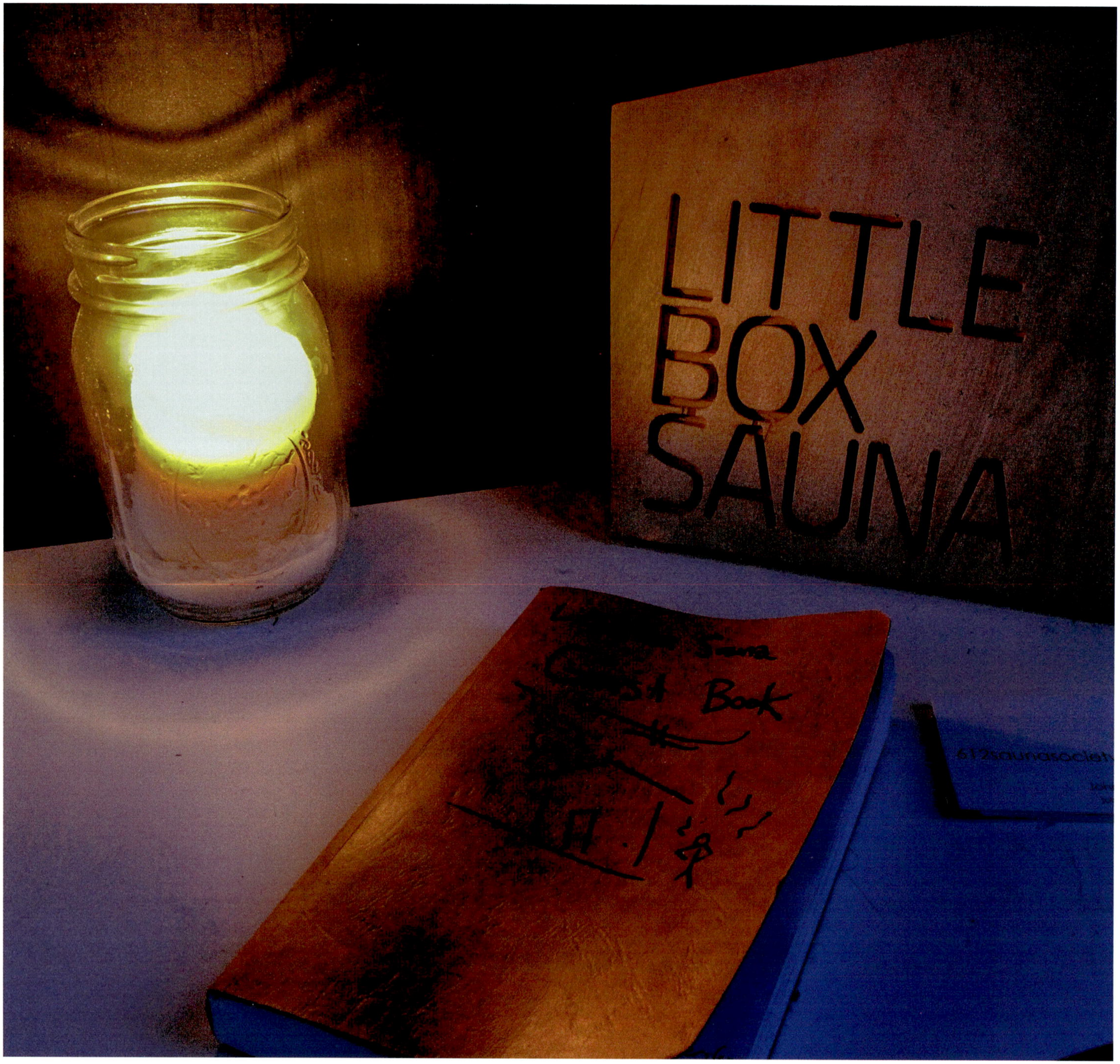
LITTLE
BOX
SAUNA

He carried the box carefully to the appointed address with the $400 shoes inside. Upon arrival, he switched his own shoes to the box and hid it, then levitated into the interview wearing the gleaming new ones. The shoes must have delivered the necessary power, because he simply *knew* he cleared any final hurdles with flying colors. After the meeting, he returned to the shoe store and, apologizing profusely, explained that, as the salesman who had fitted him observed, his odd, long, and narrow feet were indeed hard to fit, and the shoes hurt too much to keep. Given the immaculate condition of the essentially unused shoes, a return and refund were easily negotiated. Perhaps the granting board sensed an alert, creative candidate in John, for he soon found himself on a flight to Helsinki along with another successful program applicant.

They had been on Finnish soil only a few minutes when their first host, Jussi Hermunen, whisked them off toward his home and family. Knowing the rigors of a long ocean-crossing flight, Jussi did what any gracious Finnish host would do. He pulled into a convenient public sauna to ensure that the plane's recycled air and cramped quarters would be steamed from his guests' muscles and memories. John and his companion had heard of sauna, and had even experienced the substandard versions that are often part of hotels and gyms in the States. Unsure of protocols in Finland, the two left their undershorts on, but Jussi quickly suggested, "Boys, take your trunks off. It will be easier."

As they entered the hot room, a handful of stout Finns made space on the benches, and Jussi fell into conversation with them. At one point, John saw some sly smiles among the men, who, to that point, had been unexpressive. They began to ladle water to the rocks with increased frequency, keeping it up until the resulting *löyly* forced the boys to bolt to the cooling area. Behind them, the little room roared with laughter. When

John Pederson.

they returned, Jussi switched to English. "Welcome to Finland," he bade them.

John may not have known it at the time, but the axis of his world had tilted. As authentic sauna can, the experience proved utterly profound and perpetually revealing. Sauna would remain central.

John later settled in Minneapolis, where he took a job managing a web design company. One day, Jesse a graphic designer he was meeting with, mentioned the rise of the Tiny House movement, which was just gaining momentum. So enthusiastic was Jesse about his new interest that he offered to take John to see a few suburban examples. The Tiny House movement was appealing in reflecting a less-is-more philosophy, offering sustainability and affordability to those with debt loads or a need to live in otherwise expensive surroundings. In addition, many were small enough to be built on trailer beds, offering a nomadic option. John was smitten—so smitten that when the two passed an unfinished shed in someone's yard, John jumped out and offered to buy it.

With the deal concluded, John said he'd return with a trailer to pick up the shed. Craig's List solved that oversight, and he soon found himself the proud owner of a used twin-axle flat-bed trailer and the beginnings of a building. Being a gregarious collaborator by nature, he reached out to the tiny house community, and builder Jim Wilkins author of *Tiny Green Cabins*, came into the picture. Jim needed web design as much as John needed tiny house guidance. A trade was made. Jim's knowledge came complete with a crew that included welders, carpenters, and a Bobcat forklift for heavy lifting. The retrofitting of shed and trailer began.

It soon became apparent that the project was more complicated than building fresh from the axles up might have been, but it was exciting and fun, and the crew was happy to work with what it had. John didn't have a fully formed idea of what his emerging tiny house would encompass, but he reveled in the opportunity to work with his hands as balance to a job largely in front of a computer screen. Of course, web design demanded most of his time, and after the initial burst of crew-supported work concluded, progress slowed considerably on the project. He began to imagine the structure's ground floor as a mobile office and, with sleeping quarters in the loft, he would have a fine and versatile retreat.

As work continued, a small community coalesced around the project, and Glenn Auerbach, who lived a short distance away, got wind of it. Glenn publishes an online newsletter called *Sauna Times*, and had written an ebook about building his own sauna. He had been directly involved with the creation of at least twelve new neighborhood sauna projects, and John's sauna-sized tiny house had instant appeal.

Glenn's influence caused John's thinking to take a turn and adopt a new trajectory and target. The combined office, micro-kitchen, and micro-bathroom ideas that had been percolating were abandoned in favor of a sauna. The sauna stove would heat the up-ladder bedroom, and the cooling/changing room would double as living space. The sauna would serve both friends and community. However, the community aspect stretched these ideas. Why not open this further? He declared a Sauna Awareness Month, which Glenn's publication gave wider voice to. Friends and friends of friends reached out to others looking for a sauna experience. John became skilled as host and ambassador for all things sauna. The tiny house origins had fallen away and in its place, Firehouse Sauna was born.

John then founded the 612 Sauna Society as a means of communication and providing a forum for a growing number of enthusiasts. The society takes its name from the area code for Minneapolis. As such, one must say "six, one, two," rather than compressing it to "six-twelve." Occasionally, the Firehouse Sauna took up residency in a friend's driveway in a different part of town, expanding the reach and accommodating the growing tribe of people following the sauna and its burgeoning online interest group.

Web design began to take up less of John's time given his new obsession, and he stopped courting new clients. Simultaneously, Firehouse Sauna and 612 Sauna Society gained traction and speed, taking on lives of their own. Somehow in the flurry of evolving activity, other stars in a growing constellation of people with convergent interests made themselves known.

Various people known to John and Glenn, along with those who emerged via the 612 Sauna Society, began to take on leading roles. Where initial work often coincidentally took place on parallel tracks, the newer roles became ever more choreographed and deliberate. Each

Glenn Auerbach enjoying the heat in Firehouse Sauna.

character brought a skill to the table, and ideas became visionary and collaborative. In the subsoil around the taproot of traditional sauna, a number of smaller rootlets expanded and encountered each other, pooling nutrients and inexorably preparing to push a revival of public sauna within the city into view above ground.

The view forward was characterized by inclusiveness and community outreach. Every aspect of practical work was infused with optimism flowing from a collective of generous hearts. Among those was designer Molly Reichert.

Molly grew up in a family with an electric sauna in the basement. She had also been a camper at Camp Widjewagen in Ely at the edge of the Boundary Waters Canoe Area Wilderness. Widjy, as it is affectionately known, is a famed traditional canoeing camp where forays in the Boundary Waters and adjacent Quetico Provincial Park for younger campers may lead to serious summer-long expeditions in the boreal wilderness and barren lands of Canada for those who build their skills and passion by returning year after year. The camp, like most in northern Minnesota, has a much-revered sauna.

After returning from graduate school at University of California, Berkeley, Molly joined the Architecture Department faculty at the University of Minnesota. Back in her home state, in the epicenter of Nordic bath culture, sauna was never far from her thoughts.

In 2012 she retrofitted a 1960s vintage Airstream trailer into a mobile sauna, which became known as *Tönö Sauna* (Finnish for Sauna Shack). The retrofit was part of a design and art initiative called the Art Shanty Project. The "shanty" inspiration was drawn from the ice fishing shacks that spring up on the frozen lakes in the northern tier states across America and the Canadian provinces. The project not only focused on transforming fishing shacks into art spaces, but also aimed to draw on the communal aspects of these seasonal villages that embraced winter rather than hiding from it, and to get a broader group of people outside enjoying the temporary shanty villages on ice.

A signature feature of Tönö Sauna is the curvilinear CAD/CAM fabricated benches that reflect Molly's skills as designer. The ergonomic sweep of the benches is

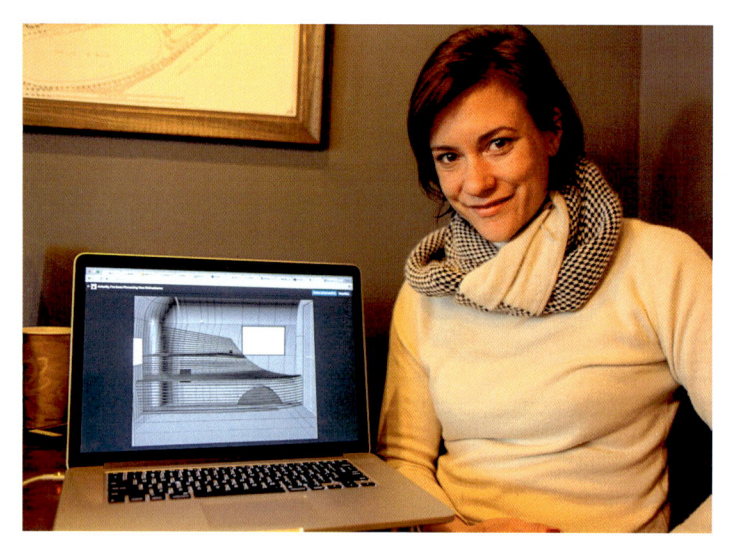

Molly Riechert.

Molly and her curvy bench masterpiece in Tönö Sauna.

reminiscent of sinuous fish as well as the sensuousness of human form and flow and the sculptural aspects of bodies. Beyond balancing the artistic with the practical elements of physical design is the equally important realm of the social and community flow facilitated by Tönö Sauna. Positive, safe, profoundly relaxing and healthful interaction among everyone is an invaluable gift when the deep cold of winter can create a feeling of isolation—even in a city. The presence of a mobile sauna brings out the best in all, especially in its ability to appear in underserved areas and to introduce sauna culture to places that might not otherwise have ready access. Appearing on the ice among fishing shacks and art shanties was just one of many imaginative forays made by Tönö Sauna.

It wasn't long before a fortuitous meeting between John Pederson and Molly Reichert occurred on sauna benches within the 612 area code region and another such meeting took place. Andrea Johnson joined the faculty of the University of Minnesota Architecture Department fresh from New York City where she had access to a number of public Russian *banyas* and Turkish baths. She was shocked that a place as large and diverse as Minneapolis seemed bereft of public bathing opportunities, especially with its proximity to the heart of North American sauna country.

Andrea grew up in South Dakota, but her mother was Minnesotan and the family would skip across the border to a family lake-edge camp. Being of Swedish heritage in the northern Midwest, it was impossible not to be immersed in sauna culture. Her affinity for sauna didn't diminish when college opportunities lured her to the Bay Area of California, where, as an undergraduate, she enrolled in urban studies with a concentration in architecture. Being a literary sort, she simultaneously engaged in a minor in poetry. Graduate school in New York was in architecture, and with the completion of that program she emerged a fully licensed architect. Once back in Minnesota, Andrea became close with Molly, professionally and through their shared passion for sauna. John dubbed them the "Sauna Mavens."

Based on the success of Tönö Sauna, Molly and Andrea hatched a scheme for another mobile sauna, and dreaming was replaced with serious designs emerging from their drafting tables. What would become known as Little Box Sauna was born, and Molly and Andrea found themselves spending as much time writing grant proposals as in the early construction phases. Fortunately, there were many ways they could both engage their students in the project for credit and benefit from an increased labor pool that didn't deplete the budget by soaking up wages. In an even greater stroke of luck, Andrea's father became willingly consumed by the project. Somehow he folded time to work on the mobile sauna around his work as a music instructor. Better yet, he had all sorts of fabrication

Andrea Johnson with early planning sketches for Little Box Sauna.

and building skills to apply to tasks and solving engineering problems as needed. It was not unusual for a twelve-hour workday to pass in the course of such enthusiastic concentration.

Connections from the bench of John's Firehouse Sauna led to another group of folks with organizational and entrepreneurial skills. As the enterprise's complexity increased, the need for additional expertise became apparent. Planners, grant writers, donors, and all manner of cooperating individuals and agencies needed enlisting to complete what was already well underway. Enter Max Musicant.

Max is a sauna regular who also happens to be the principal behind the Musicant Group. The group's mission is simple: "Creating places people want to be." What is not so simple is to describe the diversity of Max's services, and the diversity of organizations, landlords, and businesses that might benefit from his multi-disciplined approach to improving physical, social, and psychological space for maximum benefit.

Whether Max is involved in a tiny alcove, a room, a lobby, a building, a vacant lot, a park or greenspace, a city block, or a network of communities, his approach is essentially the same. What do people want? Who and what can be served? How do all forms of traffic flow? Can easy as well as unconventional alliances be forged? Can multiple uses share infrastructure in a frictionless manner? Not only does he need to know what questions to ask of a given place, he also needs to be open and receptive to questions such places might ask of him, or reveal as answers, should he be imaginative and sensitive enough.

In addition to the practical skills of creating space and the charismatic building of cooperative alliances, Max employs the perspectives of an ecologist to his projects. This brings his urban planner competence to an inspired level of holistic genius. He describes three components common to his vision in creating places people want to be. Such places are characterized by providing "choice" to individuals. Can I go? Is access clear and public? Is it safe? Does the community of users radiate trust and goodwill? Can I move things or myself around to achieve the feeling of everything being "just right?"

Secondly, Max is interested in what he calls dynamic transitions and borders. In nature, these might be seen where woodland changes to marsh and marsh changes to open water—or boreal forest transitions into open tundra, or woodland to prairie, or ocean to estuary. Typically, these borders reinforce the uniqueness of the habitat on each side, even while simultaneously binding them together. The transitions themselves often provide a shared diversity that is richer than that supported by the bioregions on either side.

The third element is attraction. What is the draw, the focus, the experience? Is it in isolation or in combination with other opportunities?

Sauna addresses and embodies each of these points specifically and superbly. With Molly and Andrea's mobile sauna having transitioned from dream and design into physical presence, Max was quick to become a sponsor and facilitator. John Pederson became an exuberant host and ambassador. Glenn Auerbach was delighted with a new evolving topic to profile in *Sauna Times*. Without courting media coverage deliberately, Little Box Sauna has generated its own gravitational field. A feature story on the cover of the Sunday *Star Tribune* revealed the aura of Little Box to the greater Minneapolis/St. Paul metropolitan region. Soon after, a local television station aired a profile on the revival of public sauna in the Twin Cities.

By the time the growing force field emanating from Minneapolis reached me in Maine, inspiring me to come see for myself, Little Box Sauna was experiencing the heady accelerated rush of a grand idea taking off. During the previous winter, the Little Box experiment had proven viable and exciting, generating a delighted constituency and increasing demand. That first season it offered free saunas while parked near the Mall of America, IKEA, and Radison Blu—cultural fixtures of big box superstores that provided the contrast and humor to the name Little Box Sauna. Earlier in the season of my visit, it had been parked near the Nicollet Mall on space provided by the Westminster Presbyterian Church. Each Little Box location seemed to contain a surprising transition, interesting contrast, or some combination of features central to the Musicant recognition of "edge."

John Pederson proved happy to meet my flight and, as lunch time was approaching, we stopped at a café on the way into town. Before we finished the meal, we discovered that our temperaments, philosophical leanings, and humor meshed as if we were long-lost brothers. Soon after he showed me to a spare room in his apartment and introduced me to his Firehouse Sauna, we stoked up the stove. Once smoke billowed from the chimney, he texted a few friends regarding my arrival in case they could join us on short notice. While the sauna heated we descended the driveway and crossed a quiet residential street to where hardwoods leaned gracefully over Minnehaha Creek. The creek snakes through Minneapolis as a riparian greenspace, with bike and pedestrian paths on each side, until it eventually joins the Mississippi River. John re-opened a hole in the ice with an axe and placed an orange traffic cone next to it to alert skiers and fat-tire bike riders traveling on the frozen surface to the small circle of open water. Snow was falling, and every 90 seconds or so a decelerating jet passed overhead on final approach to the runways of Lindbergh Field. Had I known where to look a few hours earlier, I might have seen the Firehouse Sauna adjacent to the winding creek from the air.

Margie Weaver, a woman of grace and regal bearing wrapped in a sarong, joined us on the bench. She kindly helped me get around during my visit, as her yoga teaching schedule permitted. Moments later, Glenn Auerbach of the *Sauna Times* joined us, animated by a scheme bubbling from his entrepreneurial mind. While the idea was his, he inclusively referred to "we" as if we were members of a convened design team. "We need to have troxers," he said, before charging on with the details. To his mind, troxers were a combination of swim trunks and boxer shorts, to be worn anywhere saunas required coverage. They'd be made of light, fast drying, unrestrictive fabric that wouldn't cling, be comfortable wet or dry, in sauna and outside, and could be worn in public. In combination with a sports bra or swimsuit top, they would work for women too. "For the spontaneous swimmer in us," he said. "They probably already exist, but we won't worry about that. What we need are colorful stylish options with a logo, and we'll market them through sauna shops."

"I need a pair now, for the cold-plunge in the creek," I said.

"John will loan you something. You're right, time to cool, let's go," was Glenn's response.

John did loan me something, and we trailed down the driveway to the creek in the wake of Glenn's irrepressible enthusiasm. Bemused passing drivers slowed to marvel at our procession—as red as boiled lobsters and steaming ferociously into cold air and falling snow. Various bundled-up dog walkers, bicyclists, and spandex-clad runners paused, laughed, and chatted as we enjoyed our cooling plunge. The hilariousness of contrasts was a natural conversation starter.

Daylight faded that first day, and John mentioned that we'd have supper at the house that his former sweetheart Abigail had recently purchased. A number of regulars who enjoyed the Firehouse Sauna would gather for a potluck and to help dream up the conversion of one bay of the two-car garage into a sauna. We convened in the cold garage to assess dimensions and the existing structure to be incorporated, and to get a sense of needs for a full retrofitting. Ideas flowed, and as the cold penetrated we retreated to the warm kitchen for appetizers and wine before supper. Large sheets of paper appeared and a cascade of thoughts began to surface as sketches. Our host, Abby, did not waste time when an idea unfolded, and her partner Oriel kept anything too fanciful in check with his builder/carpenter's knowledge of structural practicalities. As the sketches grew more elaborate, he kept a running list of materials and lumber requirements.

A few days later, an amusing thread of text messages and photographs emerged in real time while Abby and Oriel were in Home Depot buying materials in the company of a friendly employee, who was helpful but unfamiliar with sauna-building particulars. At the same time, Glenn Auerbach return-texted detailed advice from his office. To the employee's amazement, Glenn's instructions often included the specific aisle locations where goods peculiar to sauna construction could be found. The entire outing and exchange provided wonderful fodder for a posting on the 612 Sauna Society's web page, to inspire everyone dreaming of creating their own sauna, and who might benefit from a gentle, exemplary nudge.

The next morning a knock came on the Firehouse Sauna door while John and I enjoyed a dark-roast coffee in the cooling room/living space. David Washington entered bearing a gift he'd been working on. At first glance, it looked like a standard sauna thermometer and hygrometer mounted on a varnished cedar board. But an accompanying box of micro-electronics, circuit boards, and David's laptop quickly revealed the advent of something more elaborate.

David had been a college roommate of John's before heading to Seattle as a young wizard for Microsoft. Recently returned to Minneapolis, he had fallen under the spell of the 612 Sauna Society. He arrived prepared to program and test components to wirelessly transmit data from a sauna hot room to the gauges mounted on the cedar board, and to broadcast sauna conditions to anyone wanting to tune in vicariously. The data postings would appear on either the 612 Sauna Society webpage or the Little Box Sauna page, depending on from which hot room the transmitter was broadcasting.

While such a device might be convenient for monitoring readiness of a backyard sauna from elsewhere in one's house, John's idea was focused on outreach, and on generating interest and excitement from the greater community of followers. It wasn't long before we headed to the Blackbird Café on the corner of Nicollet and 38th streets. The Blackbird Café and the Bang Bang Hair Salon next door generously provided parking space for Little Box Sauna during January, and were among the sponsors and cooperating groups at this location. We ordered lunch while David worked at programming components to communicate with each other. The cedar board would be displayed at the end of the bar, where patrons could marvel at the temperature inside the Little Box just a hundred yards away. Gili, one of the Blackbird staff, asked if there was a walk-in policy. She thought she'd like to try it after her shift.

"You bet," John said. "Just come by and check. I always leave a space or two for walk-ins and sometimes there is a cancellation that a waiting list person doesn't snap up right away."

"Good, I'll be there," she said.

"See you on the bench!"

The Little Box Sauna is beautiful in an understated way. Architects Molly and Andrea outdid themselves in working within the linear constraints of a trailer. The angles and shapes are snug, pleasing to the eye, and reflective of multiple practical needs. The cedar cladding of the exterior is dark, achieved through the Japanese practice known as *Yaki Sugi*, literally "charred cedar." The charring process brings out the grain, results in a silvery-black tone, and is rot, insect, and fire resistant.

The overall effect is most attractive. Angles and planes are reminiscent of small outbuilding saunas: the *Yaki Sugi* effect speaks of heat and even hints at the darkened wood that characterizes the interiors of *sauvusauna*, or smoke sauna—the Finnish tradition that predates the advent of steel stoves and vent pipes.

A door graces each side of the Little Box to favor the best stair and railing placement in relation to how each parking site influences flow and use of space. The immediate courtyard serves as the cooling area, and central to that is an iron container for a wood fire people can gather around and several chairs and hay bales for seating. Here, arrivals for each ninety-minute session can collect and wait for the dressing rooms to clear for their shift. It is a friendly, welcoming place full of conversations among revelers and curious passersby wondering at the glee of swimsuit and towel-clad folks steaming in the cold, and those waiting for the shift between sessions, who, like themselves, are bundled in down outerwear and scarves.

Ascending the steps, one enters a space with two changing rooms delineated by cloth privacy drapes on one side and a door to the hot room on the other. There is just enough room along the dividing wall for a narrow bench with Little Box Sauna information on it and a selection of loaner flip-flops underneath for those who have forgotten something to keep bare feet off the cooling area pavement.

A drinking water dispenser and cups offer hydration to anyone who neglected to bring a personal water bottle.

The area in front of whichever access door is not in use provides space for a barrel containing a selection of men's and women's loaner swimsuits for serendipitous walk-in revelers who arrive unprepared. It is sturdy enough to double as a centrally located seat for the sauna host on duty.

The changing rooms provide privacy for shedding street clothes and suiting up for sauna. Each room is big enough for two at a time in the case of couples or friends willing to share, thus speeding the flow of departures and arrivals between shifts. A hinged-lid bench spans the back of the changing rooms, providing storage and seating. Above each bench are a series of ceiling hooks with a corresponding woven palm-frond satchel for each guest to store clothes. There is space for ten at a time in the hot room, and the occasional changing room chaos during session shifts is a small inconvenience for the bliss of the bench.

The hot room is glorious. A large LP gas-fired stove sits just inside to the right, easily heating the room to 180 degrees. The ceiling slopes from its high point at the stove end of the room to its lowest over the end benches. For those inside, this configuration maximizes the heat above the benches at the greatest distance from the stove. Outside, two more practicalities are realized. That end corresponds to the front end of the trailer, and the long slope forward reduces the wind-resistance when the trailer is being towed, a point that delivers increasing rewards at higher speeds of travel. Additionally, the long slope above the hot room and the shorter slope in the opposite direction above the changing rooms ensure that rain and melting snow drain completely and easily away.

Two rippled polycarbonate windows admit daylight along each wall, adding a feeling of spaciousness to an otherwise small room, yet the ripples preclude a clear view. They are simultaneously expansive and private. And the material is such that when one leans on the one along the top bench it is never so hot as to burn or startle. Likewise, all doors have such windows, and a sense of spaciousness prevails. After dark, a number of battery-powered LED lights can be moved to where they are needed most. A shapely piece of wood placed in front of the hot-room light softens the beam to a more subtle and soothing glow, while lighting in the changing room is bright enough to keep track of personal stuff. A real candle flickers on the information bench where the Little Box Sauna guest book awaits, along with business cards with links for reservations and additional information.

It is five below zero in the lot when John and I arrive to fire up for the Friday evening sessions. A fair amount of prep must be done and he is grateful to have a helper. With the heat building, we turn our attentions to unlocking the porta-potty situated behind the Little Box (in an effort to reduce the impact of its lack of aesthetics), starting the "campfire" and neatening up the courtyard. While we sweep and swab down the changing room, we discuss how best to approach my sudden appearance as photographer and journalist. John suggests introducing my project and me during his welcoming remarks to each group, giving folks a few minutes to ponder their comfort levels and wishes with this surprise addition. When they meet me in person inside, they can let me know how participatory they wish to be, or if they would prefer not to appear in any images or be quoted. We also decide John will inform me of any such wishes as a courteous double-check in case there is a communication slip-up in the greeting and changing room flow.

By the time the drinking water dispenser is filled and positioned, and our final touches for a neat and welcoming presentation are completed, we can hear the voices of people arriving for the 5:30 to 7 p.m. session. John exits to assume his role as sauna meister for the evening, and I leap for a changing room to get into a terrycloth "modesty skirt."

Through the walls I can hear John welcoming and introducing everyone while going over the Little Box points of etiquette, best strategies, and tips for enjoying sauna to newcomers. After introductions, a couple of repeaters proceed directly to the changing rooms. Within minutes, the good cheer of everyone fills the space and all of us are swept up in the looping turns of conversations or basking quietly as the moments present themselves.

In the course of the evening's three sessions, thirty-four participants share the bench. Only one or two prefer not to participate in the book project, while the rest are so agreeable and enthusiastic that they place no restrictions on what I might do with either imagery or narrative. That pattern is to prevail throughout the days ahead, and if I was already certain before that sauna magic brought out the best in people, I was completely overwhelmed by that magic as magnified by the effervescent new friends rallying at the Little Box.

Around the fire during the first cooling session, the conversation swings to the presence of the Little Box and Sauna Meister John Pederson, or JP as he's known in the abbreviated syntax of text messages and emails regarding reservations. As the prominent host, JP is the face of the collective behind the Little Box Sauna. He accepted the gratitude for all behind the project. There is no mistaking the glow and reverence in everyone's voices.

"Without John and the Little Box, I don't know what I'd do this winter."

"Me neither. Winter makes us retreat into work and home life, into our own heads. This brings me out."

"I had no idea about this. It's like a dream. A big, really big dream."

"I thought I'd probably like it, but it's bigger than that. It's like … like … I didn't know it would make my whole life happy."

Nikki, anticipating the bliss of the bench at the courtyard "campfire" while waiting for the changing room to clear between Little Box shifts.

Back inside, a few folks find commonality. They are each new parents. Stories about the mysteries, amusements, frustrations, and chronic lack of sleep ensue. And then a discovery:

"My husband is signed up for tomorrow night. I'll have kid duty then. We have a seven-month old."

"That's how my wife and I are doing it! We have a three-month- and a two-year-old. She came here last time."

During cooling sessions and between shifts, JP scampers among us, all smiles and handshakes as befits an ambassador. He greets those arriving for the next shift, keeps the introductions and flow into and out of the changing rooms smooth, leaps to the questions and curiosities of people walking by who find the sight of radiant steaming people in bathing suits, towels, and sarongs on a downtown sidewalk in winter too intriguing to ignore. If the timing and pace are such that there will be no disruption, JP shows some the interior, even the hot room, if they agree to look in quickly so that no heat escapes.

"What is this?"

"How can I reserve a seat?"

"Hey, I just read about this in the paper. Amazing!"

"How cool is this? I'm gonna try it!"

As people depart, I hear JP's cheerful, now familiar line: "See you on the bench." It is the same phrase he signs his correspondence with, and it appears at the bottom of each notification on the website. I expect it to become annoying as repetitions accumulate, but instead

Little Box participants cooling around the courtyard fire. Minus 15 degrees F in Minneapolis that night, 180 in the sauna.

it carries all the pleasures of a musical refrain. Before the week is out, I catch myself saying it as often to my new friends of the bench as they say it to me.

Connections and insights are not limited to the sauna itself. Around the fire conversations continue to swirl in their own orbits. Each time a chunk of wood is added, sparks spiral upward. Scraps of thought seem to filter into view and settle from subtle shifts and inputs from the unfolding of these 612 days. I've come from covering saunas and their people in mostly rural areas where space provides privacy, landscapes bespeak known calm, and mostly middle-aged and older people reflect sensibilities that are settled and content. Those old enough to pre-date the internet era and the consuming world of wireless devices are already practiced choosers of when and how much to engage with those options.

The imaginative childhoods of this older group have taught them how to self start, create fun and context from their own competencies, and appreciate the values of reflective time, quiet, solitude, and independence. That generation's coming of age in the "question authority" era has instilled a useful level of immunity to the tyranny of the negative aspects of peer pressure—and ever-more sophisticated and sinister marketing strategies steering us to accumulate unnecessary stuff. No great leaps have been required for this group to embrace sauna as reflective of life and conducive to mental and physical health.

Those stepping stones to sauna traditions were visible through personal observation, even in the absence of direct heritage or introduction.

Now that I've been introduced to Max and his cognizance of transitions and edges, I see them everywhere. The drama and obviousness of juxtapositions are amplified in this evolving urban sauna scene. Almost everyone is younger. The public saunas of older times have aged out, faded with the advent of small in-house electric units that became affordable in the economic boom times following World War II and the resulting "baby boom" from which those of us in the "Boomer generation" get our label. The millennials and younger folks who gravitate to the Little Box Sauna must make a far greater leap across boundaries. For those born after the hyper-connected wireless-device-driven world accelerated to fever pitch, any pause to choose something not of that world is much harder to grasp. The irony of omnipresent connectedness is that it can be simultaneously isolating. Somehow those who have fallen under the spell of the Little Box Sauna can see this—almost as if a prism were bending the light enough for an older wisdom to prevail. The younger friends on the bench have rediscovered community, trust, conversation, and the joys of slowing down to balance the demands of an accelerated world. They are choosing to park the mobile devices that got them their reservations outside with their street clothes for an hour and a half of rejuvenation and unfettered connection

Little Box revelers introducing themselves to one another at the start of a session.

with an egalitarian tribe of like-minded souls. They have reached backward to find their futures in an old, refined communal tradition.

None of this surprises Glenn Auerbach. "Those kids need this way more than we do. They need the balance," he says, articulating what is, to me, an amazing recognition. For thousands of years, sweat-bathing cultures have evolved to provide a life-affirming, health-building, world-view-illuminating retreat for physical, mental, and spiritual rejuvenation. That hasn't changed. What has changed is the world we occupy. The value of sauna traditions that have been here all along is increasing. As Glenn says, "It doesn't matter where this mobile sauna is parked, next to a big box store, or a fantastic high-rise, or in some neighborhood, it is always a refuge and contrast, a safe space of retreat and something like a nugget of purity and 'wildness' for all. That is all obvious at a lake-edge sauna up north, yet much harder to see and feel here in the city."

For my part, I've been slow to see this most remarkable aspect. These contrasts and juxtapositions don't obscure the picture. They magnify it, revealing the seriousness and power of this growing wave of sauna awareness in a world that will only benefit. Just as Henry David Thoreau coined his prescient and oft-quoted phrase expressing fear that people would come to "lead lives of quiet desperation" as the industrial revolution accelerated over a century ago, the youngest members of the Little Box Sauna community are intuiting, or seeing directly, something that may prove similarly prophetic. One current source of "quiet desperation" might very well be that an excess of electronic information stimulation through so-called "smart" devices, and the fractured attention spans that result, are toxic at overdose levels. Time in sauna can alleviate or expel those toxins. The older sauna traditions comprise the beautiful sweeping tail of a comet that keeps reappearing throughout the ages. The bright spot is whatever new and perhaps unanticipated evolutions are visible here and now. Who knows what the cascade of light at the leading edge will show us next?

Former high school classmates enjoy a surprise encounter on the Little Box bench after being out of touch during the ten years since graduating.

A group of friends booked a session as a birthday present to one among them.

Eventually the people in the last shift cool and put their clothes back on. They linger around the dwindling fire or head off toward home or a meal. Many exchange phone numbers and email addresses, discovering they are neighbors or that they met when trick-or-treating with their kids last Halloween. While I've been thinking for a while that it has been getting late, I have to remind myself that by city nightlife standards, evening is just receding and the night is young. After neatening up and putting the Little Box to bed, JP and I walk to a nearby Japanese establishment. He is happily tired, but still a little wired from being "on" as host. I tell him how moving it was to feel everyone's heartfelt comments as they departed. "They love you," I say. "Some of them said so, and you absorbed enough handshakes, hugs, kisses, and fist-bumps to run for mayor."

The barkeep greets John warmly, the way staff at all the local establishments do when the Little Box is parked in their vicinity. He doesn't charge us for our shots of heated sake or for a slice of cheesecake. I order a meal, having skipped supper to cover for John while he dashed to the Blackbird for a quick bite once things were going smoothly at Little Box.

The festive intensity of good will was so inspiring that it actually took a toll on me. I didn't recognize this accumulating fatigue until Margie Weaver picked me up and we drove over to St. Paul in response to an invitation from Connie Kauppi to visit her sauna and stay for supper. Short as the drive was, I kept falling asleep at any lull in our conversation.

Once a month, Connie provides a big meal and fires up for a bunch of regulars. Her sauna is a tiny stand-alone in her back yard, complete with a Finnish flag hung on the outside of the changing room. Connie is boisterous, welcoming, and quick to laugh. Her sauna is snug and made with attention to detail. There is a very small changing room, and a narrow hot room longer than it is wide. The top bench is deep, maybe four feet or so. If you lean on the back wall your feet just reach the edge facing the stove. You can toast the soles of your feet nicely. Three can fit on the top bench with each leaning on a wall. The lower bench would allow two more, but more often it is used as a foot rest for people perched on the edge of the top bench for maximum heat.

Connie prefers to let her guests figure out their own experience and limits her instructional comments to making sure that they heat and cool several times, and drink plenty of water. Because of the tiny dimensions, people flow in and out over a longer period throughout the evening. Margie and I were able to dissolve into a lovely quiet basking session, and I enjoyed a much-appreciated solo session after that—a wonderful contrast to the centrifugal social whirl of the Little Box.

As with all limited visits to a place, time seems to both speed up and compress as the final hours approach. I was fortunate to meet Max Musicant on the bench at Little Box, but there were others I would not meet. Andrea Johnson was away on business, and a few other potential contacts couldn't mesh a meeting into being as the remaining time slipped away. Fortunately, Molly Reichert was most gracious in carving out time, having just returned from her own trip. She introduced me to Tönö Sauna, parked for the winter at a friend's house. The sauna was beginning to show some wear and tear from hard use before the Little Box took over that role, but it was still marvelously serviceable. Despite teaching two courses this term, being involved in four extra-curricular projects, and running late for a dinner date, she invited me to fire up. She'd return in a few hours, and in the meantime would notify any regulars who might want to come. All that on a school night that promised to go late by the time she could return me to John's. I was grateful for her generosity.

In the 4:30 a.m. darkness on the way to the airport, John asked me a question that I happened to have a ready answer for: "Is there an encapsulating moment you can recall from your stay in the 612?"

"Yeah, there is," I replied. "Remember the night you left your daypack at the place we had gone after shutting up the Little Box, and you dashed back for it? It was pretty late; not many of those hybrid buses on Nicollet. I was looking across the intersection to where Little Box was quiet and dark when an overwhelming rush of affection for it engulfed me. It was cold, but not breezy enough for me to be tearing up—except that I was. The only thing like that is the feeling I get after leaving a contra dance in some lovely old New England Grange Hall. There's always a moment after the dancers have left, the band is packed up, and the caller has departed, when the lights blink out. If I see that happen I get hit like that; I can't help but wonder if the timbers in those buildings hold the memories of the music, the swirling skirts and rhythms of feet, and all that unbridled community happiness. Forever…"

"No wonder you totally get it," he said. Then, so softly I leaned closer to hear him, "You know, if we just fill the world with so much goodness, there is no room for evil around the edges. That's all we're really trying to do."

I thought my Minneapolis sojourn had concluded. But when JP casts a spell, it tends to linger and evolve. The following June I got a call. John said: "When are you coming back? Things are unfolding. I'll pick you up again."

Little Box thus far is a winter phenomenon. It hibernates during the warm months when people are busy with activities reserved for the longer daylight and warmth of summer. In that lull, JP simply shifted his sauna activities back to his own Firehouse Sauna, but never stopped dreaming. Analyzing statistics revealed by the Little Box season showed surprising details. More than 2,000 bench spaces had been reserved over the winter, sponsorships and income had been impressive, and momentum showed no signs of slowing. Other communities and even distant cities were asking advice on how to launch similar public sauna programs. A community in Nova Scotia launched a mobile public sauna that even looked like the Little Box.

Rather than shrink from his increasing responsibilities as sauna meister, JP began to ponder ways the growing workload might be shared. What if a sauna cooperative were created? It would give ownership to the members; communal responsibilities could be delegated as competence and willingness emerged. By September, an advisory board morphed into a board of directors. In October a fundraising campaign created and launched an effort through Kickstarter. One week before the twenty-eight-day Kickstarter program concluded in early November, the minimum goal was exceeded and success was in hand. Building another mobile sauna for Minneapolis commenced.

By early February, the gleaming new sauna was parked at Surly Brewing, sponsor and host for the month. Two stove-heated Snowtrekker tents expanded the comfort of the courtyard and cooling area, and the logo of the 612 Sauna Society was crisp and prominent on the trailer. Around the perimeter of the courtyard a number of festive red rectangles of cloth printed with the logo fluttered in the breezes like Tibetan prayer flags. Hundreds and hundreds of volunteer hours were celebrated with events at the brewery to thank the many people who had worked nights and weekends at "build parties."

While gleaming new structures are easy to appreciate and the charisma of welcoming sauna hosts a pleasure to experience, a huge amount of intensely focused work takes place in the background of every 612 Sauna Society success. It is not only less visible and frequently underappreciated, but all the more remarkable because it is volunteer, often of professional quality, and extraordinarily time consuming. Passion fuels such commitment.

Among the volunteers, Teke O'Reilly's name keeps percolating into view. Need someone to write and edit most of the promotional and organizational documents and memos? Teke's on it. Need some technical know-how in the creation and carrying out of a Kickstarter campaign? Seems like Teke has it covered. Need someone to direct all the complexities of follow-through after the fundraising success? Teke surfaces as the primary choreographer. Not only do all the needs and sequencing of requirements get met, but with amazing speed. Every so often Teke disappears completely. It usually means he is really concentrating on something.

During the final days of February, traditional sauna enthusiast Yukiko Oyama arrived to see what all the excitement was about. She divides her time between Brooklyn, New York, and Japan, and would share the expanding magic of the 612 Sauna Society at a festival in Nagano, Japan, hosted by the Japan Sauna Association during the first weekend in March. Before experiencing the joys of the 612 bench, Yuki presented gifts from the ambassador of the Japan Sauna Association, Katsuki Tanaka, to her new friends and hosts in Minneapolis. Yuki suggested that a letter of greeting be written from the 612 group to the Japan Sauna Association that she would translate and read at the annual festival the very next weekend. Not surprisingly, Teke O'Reilly proudly penned the letter.

During March, the Swedish American Institute hosted the new sauna. By then a request had been posted to suggest a name for it, and the one that received the most votes had been submitted by Sara Hill.

Sara has been involved with the re-emerging Minneapolis sauna scene from the get-go, and brings not just countless hours of volunteering, but a direct authenticity. She was raised in Duluth, her Finnish forebears lived in several of the smaller towns of the Iron Range just north of there. She understands layers from a geologist's point of view and through her personal heritage. The connections from iron ore in the ground to the trains that ship it to the edge of Lake Superior for pelletizing and shipment to the Great Lakes steel mills are not lost on her. Nor is the full circle of that finished steel coming back to several regional sauna stove manufacturers.

She was the one who volunteered to drive three and a half hours north to Tower, Minnesota, to pick up the new Kuuma stove during the final stages of the build. It's a long-enough round trip for someone of a thoughtful and literary bent to ponder naming possibilities. She even paused to rescue a bewildered stray dog by the highway and, by posting on social media, return it to a grateful owner during the southbound return to Minneapolis. All the way back the dog positioned itself near the new stove in the rear of the van as if such a precious cargo might benefit from guarding.

Perhaps it was the spray of sparks from welder's torches at Lamppa Manufacturing where the stove was made, or the gleaming black stove paint on new steel about to become the fiery heart of the sauna that eased the idea of "The Forge" into Sara's mind. Initially, the obvious symbols presented themselves, such as friends who participated in the build-parties who had forged an alliance on various sauna benches in the 612, or the specifics of the project forging ever tighter community bonds. But then she reached deeper. The cadence of tires on tar of her road trip through the Iron Range may have meshed with the cadence of the long epic poem of sorcerers and shamans of *Kalevala*, the famous saga of Finnish origins.

Kalevala for centuries had been an oral tradition often accompanied by the music of the *kantele*. In the 1840s, written versions began appearing, and despite periodic attempts at squelching by various hierarchical religions that find its candor, juiciness, and mysticism too compelling and interesting for their strictures, its glory and lyricism persist. It has been translated into more than thirty languages.

Among the heroes of the *Kalevala* is Ilmarinen, a supernatural blacksmith. After discovering iron, Ilmarinen comes to understand the forging of iron into bright steel. Persuasion and a bit of trickery bring him to "the forging of the Sampo," a magical mill that grinds food and salt and mints coins. He has help. Guidance comes from a "golden spruce," the moon, and "the Great Bear shining in the heavens." Extra incentive is for the hand of a maiden. Mere mortals cannot pump the bellows of his forge powerfully enough to create the beautiful Sampo. All four winds are enlisted "to the utmost of their power."

Sara harnessed all this in conjuring the name The Forge. Those of us who checked the box for the vote intuited a bigger story and greater meanings in the generous cascade of sparks falling from Ilmarinen's mighty hammer and Sara's vision. In the small ways that are the province of mortals, we gave our blessings to the processes and evolutions of the 612 Sauna Society and the peace-building community it fosters. What could be more noble than sharing communal grace for the benefit of all through authentic sauna?

And what could be more encompassing than a name that honors a mythical smithy from the country of origin, yet forges ahead across oceans and cultures and generations to invite one and all to show up, slow down, and revel in the infinite benefits and beauties of Finland's greatest gift to the world?

A journalist from Minnesota Monthly interviews John Pederson just before folks arrive for a firing of The Forge.

The tent sauna offered by Snowtrekker Tents of Wisconsin is double-walled for heat retention, has more elaborate heat shielding for stove placement and pipe passage through the wall than their standard trail tents, yet incorporates all the advantages and conveniences of internal framing and breathable canvas.

Mobile Saunas: Often Practical, Always Fun

While plenty of practicalities and niceties are highlighted by The Forge, Little Box Sauna, and Tönö Sauna in Minneapolis, the idea of mobile saunas is older and more widespread than one might suspect. No great leaps of imagination are required for inspiration, and saunas onboard ships, trains, and all manner of runnered, tracked, and wheeled vehicles no doubt quickly followed the advent of such things. Novelty and humor have inspired a sauna in tramway cars of several European ski areas, and a variety of functional vehicles retrofitted as saunas bring the idea of mobility into the realm of a drivable sauna. A number of companies provide tent saunas that can be pitched anywhere, limited only by ambition and a willingness to pack them to a chosen site.

There are several annual rendezvous in Europe and North America where people convene to showcase their inventiveness with mobility. A couple of books and calendars celebrate the variety of mobile units that range from official Finnish military vehicles to the most whimsical of artful trailers and even a retrofitted VW bus painted as if it flew through a time-warp straight from a 1970s concert. During 2017, the one-hundred-year anniversary of Finland's independence, a collaboration of Finnish American groups promoted sauna and Finnish culture via a mobile sauna that toured the United States for the entire year.

Interesting and fun as all mobile variations may be, with practicalities that are easy to appreciate, there are certain conditions that may inspire slightly subversive strategic possibilities. As zoning laws become more restrictive and complicated, mobile saunas may provide a way to legally sidestep overly prescriptive clauses that, while well-intentioned, may prevent the building of a permanent sauna even if it is under the square footage threshold for requiring a building permit and is essentially simple and small enough to be free of real impact.

There are some lovely water-edge saunas that are old enough to predate current regulations and are "grandfathered" into being, but such examples are no longer common and new ones will not replace them in most situations. Many have decks that extend over the water for cold-plunge access. Some are actually built at the end of docks above the water surface. A few straddle streams where the sound of rushing water is part of the interior experience and access to a cooling plunge is literally at the doorstep. With few remote unregulated exceptions, such options are seldom available to those building a new structure. The closer to more densely populated areas, the more elaborate restrictions tend to be, and the fewer exceptions likely to be granted.

Even where there are totally acceptable zoning ordinances one might agree with, there is often a wish for reasonable exceptions. A case in point would be watershed protection setbacks. These are eminently sensible and necessary in the case of dwellings that involve serious site disruption, foundations, effluent, and other large-scale impacts, but the rules often include simple structures such as boathouses, sheds, and saunas. Small esthetic structures that are not dwellings might easily fall into a non-targeted category where one might hope for a reasonable waiver of the rules. In the face of denial, mobile saunas occasionally offer an acceptable alternative that both regulators and individuals can agree to.

In a best-case situation, a sauna on a trailer, floating dock, or pontoon boat may slip through the regulatory cracks without issue. In a place where a permanent structure is not allowed at all, or allowed with restrictions as to distances from property lines, the parking of a trailer may not come under such rules in the first place. Other scenarios can require a bit of dancing with the letter of the laws, and while temporary relief from enforcement may result, there is always the risk of "teaching" the regulatory committees to close such loopholes. I know of someone who has achieved a bit of success through attentiveness to language in the zoning ordinances of their area by creatively interpreting "permanent structure" and some rules regarding the edge of open water. It seems there is specific language that establishes a 120-day limit for parking a trailer next to water that is in place to accommodate a seasonal campground business offering tent and trailer sites along the edge of a local lake. Every 119 days the sauna owner diligently tows the trailer the sauna is built on the requisite 150 feet or more away from the water's edge as required for permanent structures built on the ground. On day 120, it sits idle beyond the legal remove. On day 121 it reappears at water edge for the next cycle of allowable days. The municipality doesn't waste any time revising statutes in a time- and energy-consuming game of cat and mouse, and the sauna owners get to imagine they have beat the system. No damage occurs to the watershed, and the owners enjoy a water-edge sauna. Thus far there have been no "who do you think you are" complaints from neighbors around the lake that have resulted in a cease-and-desist order.

It always pays to research the local regulations thoroughly before investing in a sauna. This is simply a best practice of community relations, and can set the stage

Photo by Alix W. Hopkins.

for good communication, courtesy, and citizenship. It also might just pay to keep the idea of a sauna on a trailer or a pontoon boat in the back of your mind just in case there is need for a legal work-around that is inoffensive and satisfies all concerned.

Tent saunas bring mobility and portability to yet another level. For those who may not want to invest in a project involving building materials and trailers, the tent option may provide a final refuge for those with real or voluntary budget constraints. In the face of restrictive regulations or neighboring malcontents who look for, find, and create trouble for anyone they perceive as getting away with something or having too much fun, a tent sauna may be the final form of resistance. They can be pitched only for the duration of use and then taken down, and thus retain maximum evasiveness by ceasing to exist as necessary.

About the Author

Garrett Conover is best known as the cofounder of North Woods Ways, the classically resonant canoe and snowshoe guiding service leading wilderness trips in Maine, Quebec, and Labrador from 1980 until 2007. Garrett is author of *Beyond the Paddle*. His novella, *Kristin's Wilderness*, has won four awards. *The Snow Walker's Companion* was coauthored with Alexandra Conover Bennett, and is now in its fourth printing. Writing and photography are continuing interests, and Garrett remains in demand as a presenter of North Woods Skills Workshops and Adventure Travel Slideshows, where the narration weaves a bit of history, how-to, natural history, and the intrigue of glorious wilderness trails into each presentation. He is currently a craftsman and fabricator at Sheldon Slate Products in Monson, Maine.

Photo by Alix W. Hopkins.